Developmental Pathogenesis
and Treatment
of Borderline and
Narcissistic Personalities

Developmental Pathogenesis and Treatment of Borderline and Narcissistic Personalities

Donald B. Rinsley, M.D., F.R.S.H.

JASON ARONSON INC.
Northvale, New Jersey
London

Library of Congress Cataloging-in-Publication Data

Rinsley, Donald B.
    Developmental pathogenesis and treatment of borderline and
    narcissistic personalities / Donald B. Rinsley.
       p.   cm.
    Includes bibliographies and index.
    ISBN 0-87668-828-8
    1. Narcissism in children—Pathogenesis. 2. Narcissism in
children—Treatment. 3. Borderline personality disorders in
children—Treatment. 4. Child analysis.   I. Title.
    [DNLM: 1. Narcissism 2. Personality Disorders—etiology.
3. Personality Disorders—therapy. 4. Psychoanalytic Therapy.   WM
460.5.E3 R582d]
RJ506.N37R56 1989
616.85′85—dc20
DNLM/DLC   89-17506
for Library of Congress   CIP

Manufactured in the United States of America. Jason Aronson Inc. offers books and cassettes. For information and catalog write to Jason Aronson Inc., 230 Livingston Street, Northvale, New Jersey 07647.

For
My Teachers, Who Have Taught Me Much
My Students, Who Have Taught Me More
and
My Patients, Who Have Taught Me the Most

Contents

Part III. Supervision

Preface

This book is about borderline and narcissistic personalities. It consists of three sections. The first section synthesizes a developmental understanding of their pathogenesis and clinical symptomatology based upon psychoanalytic principles. The second section is a discussion of certain key aspects of their treatment based on these principles. The third section presents aspects of the supervision of the psychoanalytic therapeutic process. This volume is the product of some thirty years of work with borderline and narcissistic children, adolescents, and adults, and their dysfunctional families. During these years I have served as a supervisor of psychotherapy for residents in adult psychiatry and fellows in child psychiatry (under the auspices of the Karl Menninger School of Psychiatry and Mental Health Sciences) and for pre- and post-doctoral students in clinical and counseling psychology, as well as graduate students of social work.

The book's theoretical focus combines both classical and object-relations concepts, a "mixed model" approach that reflects the sweeping changes that have taken place in psychoanalytic theory and practice during my professional lifetime. I have retained and utilized classical metapsychological principles while incorporating newer, path-blazing concepts derived from the original and creative contributions of the British School. The latter, epitomized in the works of Melanie Klein, W. R. D. Fairbairn, Michael Balint, Wilfred Bion, and D. W. Winnicott, have decisively transformed psychoanalysis from an essentially mechanistic drive-reduction theory emphasizing instinctual aim into a body of theory and praxis based on the developmental primacy of internalized and external object relations. This transformation has opened the door to a deeper and more comprehensive understanding of normal and pathological psychological development, particularly the pathogenesis and psychoanalytic treatment of borderline and narcissistic personalities. To these I add due and proper recognition of Margaret Mahler's epochal contributions to the understanding of the separation-individuation process.

No book of this kind could have been written without

major reliance on the profound and prolific contributions of Otto Kernberg, who well-nigh singlehandedly raised the profession's consciousness to a comprehension of what the borderline personality is and how it comes to be. Much is also owed to the writings of the late Heinz Kohut, who has illumined the pathogenesis of the narcissistic personality.

Finally, I owe a considerable debt to my publisher, Dr. Jason Aronson, who shepherded my two prior books through the publication process and whose urgings are largely responsible for the appearance of this one. And an inestimable degree of appreciation is accorded my wife Charlotte and my daughter Eve, whose forbearance and understanding allowed me the time to put it together.

Donald B. Rinsley
Topeka, Kansas
May 1989

PART I

DEVELOPMENTAL PATHOGENESIS

Life is short
The art long
Decision difficult
Experiment perilous
— Hippocrates of Cos

Chapter 1

Infantile Grandiosity and Helplessness

Three general assumptions underlie the following discussion of the developmental pathogenesis of borderline and narcissistic personality disorders. The first holds that these conditions share closely related pathogeneses resulting from very early (pre-oedipal) developmental arrest. The second holds that the narcissistic personality represents a more advanced or better organized (higher-level) version of the borderline personality (Adler 1981, 1985).

The third holds that these personality disorders arise as a result of significant impairment of the separation–individuation process (Mahler et al. 1975).

From the moment of birth, the infant senses that his body and its needs exist in relation to "an other" personage (Stern 1985), whom Fairbairn (1954) termed the *original object*—in most cases the natural or biological mother. Nevertheless, it is also evident that the baby's early attentive focus is predominantly limited to himself and his diffusely perceived bodily exigencies, a condition to which Freud (1914a) applied the term *primary narcissism*. Thus, the mother–infant bonding relationship, beginning *in utero* and attaining its peak intensity between the first and sixth postnatal months (Mahler's *symbiotic phase*), has as its prime objective the preservation of the infant's life. The most basic of all needs—to survive—has its most pristine expression in the mother–infant bond, and it animates and underlies all subsequent human relationships. It is generally understood that the nature and quality of the child's relationships with parents during the first several years will critically determine the major features of the child's—and later the adult's—relationships with others.

At birth and in gradually decreasing degree throughout the preschool years, the child requires outside assistance for the regulation of his basic visceral–autonomic processes. Indeed, the neonate is for some hours unable even to regulate its own body temperature. The baby is in a state of pervasive psychophysiological lability or instability: pupils dilate and constrict, the skin flushes and blanches, and mass motor discharges reflect rapidly and markedly shifting internal states. As soon as the mother takes the baby up in her arms and brings it into contact with her body, these "affectomotor storms" (Mahler 1965) quickly damp down, and the baby begins to root and suck and proceeds to feed, after which it falls asleep. On the other hand, a state of persistent affectomotor arousal significantly interferes with and consequently impairs the infant's normal feeding process and exerts a deleterious effect on the baby's quotidian rhythms, that is, its sleep–wake–feed–sleep cycle.

The mother whose ministrations to her infant effectively damp down and modulate the baby's affectomotor arousals functions as a "good breast" (Klein 1935, 1940, 1952) whose relationship with her baby is predominantly gratifying to him. Her basic benevolence and nurturance are conveyed to the infant in myriad gross and subtle ways, including her own vegetative actions and rhythms, her vocalizations, touch, bodily postures and movements, manner of feeding and handling her baby, and general emotional disposition. These interactional elements summate into an initially vague perceptual complex of a predominantly positive, gratifying (tension-easing) nature, which the infant proceeds to internalize and incorporate over time into the anlage of what will gradually take shape as a basic component of his self-identity.

The infant's primary narcissism finds its peak expression in the youngster's symbiotic relationship with the mother, approximately from the first to the sixth postnatal months, during which the earliest manifestations of Kohut's (1971, 1977) "dual track" narcissism make their appearance—the *grandiose self* and the *idealized parental image*. As Greenberg and Mitchell (1983) point out, the behav-

ioral metaphor conveyed by the grandiose self amounts to
"I am perfect and you admire me," whereas the behavioral
metaphor conveyed by the idealized parental image
amounts to "You are perfect and I am a part of you"
(p. 354). The great paradox of this developmental period
finds graphic expression in the infant's immense grandiosity (infantile megalomania) coexisting with his profound
helplessness and dependency. During this very early time,
both the grandiosity and the dependency come to be
projected into the figure of the mother and reintrojected
from her in repetitive, circular fashion as the infant endows
her with his own as yet dimly perceived characteristics. Of
immense importance is the mother's container–contained
function (Bion 1967), according to which she fields the
baby's projections, reframes and remodels them, adds to
them a scaffolding of her own cognitive processes, and
returns them to her baby, thereby endowing him with the
anlage of the capacity to think.

The infant's, and later the older child's, ongoing projection of his natural grandiosity into the mother, and later
both parents, serves the child as the basis for the development of the ego ideal (Freud 1914a), based on the child's
idealization of the parents. But to repose one's grandiosity
in others thus endows them with enormous power, including power over oneself; hence, in order for the grandiose projections to serve the purposes of healthy
maturation, or indeed to occur to any degree at all, the
parent–child relationship must be one of trust (Erikson
1963). And inasmuch as the young child's ability to cede his
infantile grandiosity to his parents represents an initial step
toward differentiating them from himself ("I am power-

ful"—"You are powerful"), early basic trust forms the basis for one's ability to sense and test reality (Frosch 1960, 1964, 1970). In turn, early basic trust reinforces the young child's ability to utilize the parents, and in particular the mother, as containers who serve to ease and modulate his affecto-motor vicissitudes.

Yet another fundamentally important experiential entity promotes the child's growth and development during this early period—the transitional object (Winnicott 1951). Coming into use by the infant on the average between four and eighteen months, the transitional object assumes many forms—a nondescript piece of cloth, a coverlet, a stuffed toy—which the child strokes, rubs, sucks, tongues, and mouths. It serves as an early not-mother object that the child utilizes for self-soothing. The transitional object also serves as an early indicator of the child's awareness that he is "not quite mother" and that he may in a limited way manipulate—hence have impact on—outside objects and events. The transitional object thus serves as an early indicator of the infant's capacity for self–object differentiation and for his nascent sense of mastery. The child's most advanced use of transitional objects is later embodied in his play with toys, which provides him with endless opportunities for the development and creative use of fantasy—the world of pretend and make believe—which further catalyzes the ongoing evolution of the child's cognitive development.

Chapter 2

The Acquisition of Internal Stability

In order to function appropriately during later childhood and fully socialized adulthood, the very young child must acquire ever-expanding skill in damping down and modulating by himself his spontaneous and frustration-related affectomotor discharges; he must acquire increasing degrees of internal self-regulation. How does the child accomplish this task? He does so by internalizing (introjecting) the parent figures, along with their self-regulating function, which is achieved by means of the development of *object constancy*.

Object constancy is comprised of cognitive-perceptual (mnemonic) and affective (emotional) elements (Fraiberg 1969) and is correctly understood to encompass both (A. Freud 1960, 1968). The mnemonic component has to do with the capacity to summon up a consistent inner image or representation of another person, that is, to have evolved from reliance on recognitory memory to the capacity for evocative memory (Beres 1968, Hartmann 1952, 1956a,b); this transformation probably begins during the last trimester of the first postnatal year (Spitz 1957), is well under way toward the end of the second year (Metcalf and Spitz 1978), and is essentially completed toward the latter half of the third year (Mahler 1965, 1968, Mahler et al. 1975). The affective or emotional component is expressed in the growing child's libidinal tie to, or emotional bonding with, the mother, which has its inception in the symbiotic phase (1–6 months), is marked by the normal stranger anxiety at 8 months (Spitz 1957), and is well developed by the middle of the second year, at roughly 18 months (Nagera 1966).

Object constancy is not to be confused with *object permanency*, a term originating with Piaget (1937). Object permanency has to do with the growing child's perceptual ability to differentiate "external" objects from his manipulation of them, to perceive them as having an existence of their own independent of him. Object permanency ordinarily develops by roughly 18 months of age. In the healthily developing, properly nurtured infant, toddler, and pre-school child, the two—object permanency and object constancy—undergo coordinated development. From the beginning, the healthy mother, optimally nurtured and assisted by her healthy spouse, provides the substrate for the child's recognition of others, then of others as separate and distinct from himself, and then for the child's capacity to summon up inner images of others, and finally to utilize these evoked images for easing and modulating the child's heretofore labile affectomotor (visceral-autonomic) discharges. All of these interrelated goings-on betoken the growing child's capacity to differentiate his self-representations ("I, Me") from object representations ("You, It"), as Kernberg (1966, 1972, 1977) has cogently pointed out.

To summarize, as these terms are defined for the purposes of this discussion, object permanency, the mnemonic component of object constancy, constitutes the ability to summon up (evoke) inner images of persons or things that are absent from one's immediate physical environment. To this object constancy adds an affective or emotional component derived from the tension-easing (drive-reducing) mother–infant bonding relationship. In concrete terms:

> *Object Permanency*: "I can remember what you look like when you're not here with me."
> *Object Constancy*: "I can remember what you look like when you're not here with me and it makes me feel good (better)."

The acquisition of increasing degrees of internal stability or self-regulation, reflected in the ability to modulate and control one's inner drive states, is intimately related to the capacity to perceive oneself as a separate and distinct being or person. Well-developed evocative memory is profoundly connected to one's sense of (separated) selfhood; at the same time, one's self-representations remain to a healthy extent connected to object-representations (Kohut's "selfobjects").

Chapter 3

The Role
of Fantasy

It may rightly be said that, if play is the child's work, fantasy is the child's world, and the two are intimately associated in the child's everyday experience. As Sarnoff (1980) notes:

> (P)lay fantasy . . . becomes a means of reducing emotional tensions . . . the symbolization of which . . . becomes a highly useful tool in the process of mastery of uncomfortable experiences and in the

discharge of drive energies for which the immature physi-
ology of the child provides no other outlets. . . . [p. 286]

Evocative memory is essential for the child's capacity to
indulge in both the tension-easing and creative outlets that
play provides, to advance the play beyond the banal exer-
cise of imageless, hence fantasy-deficient (alexithymic) au-
toerotic movements that characterize retarded and autistic
children. Again, fantasy can only serve creative intellectual
and artistic purposes if the fantasizer, fully able to sense and
test reality, voluntarily departs from that reality during
periods of self-governed creativity. To be able to do so
requires a significant degree of healthy separation.

   To summarize, evocative memory, the mnemonic-
eidetic component of object constancy, develops within the
context of good enough mothering as a consequence of the
child's progressive internalization of the mother's image,
and rather later, that of the father. In turn, the child's
progressively drive-reducing and evolving creative use of
fantasy is related to his growing ability to sense and test
reality, of which his expanding differentiation of self-
representations (self-images) and object representations
(object images) is an integral component. Adler (1985)
defines the complex mnemonic-eidetic-affective endopsychic structure that underlies and vivifies the growing child's
object constancy as the *holding introject* "(t)hat promotes in
the self a feeling of being soothingly held" (p. 17).

Chapter 4

The Separation–Individuation Process

The path-breaking observational psychoanalytic studies of Margaret Mahler and her associates at the Masters Center in New York City led to her formulation of the process of separation–individuation, of what she termed the psychological birth of the human infant (Mahler et al. 1975). The hyphenation of the term signifies the fact that there are two subprocesses involved, namely, separation and individuation.

The *separation* subprocess encompasses all those actions and experiences that signify and contribute to the growing child's awareness that he is a unique personage, a being who is different and distinct from every other thing and person, a self apart from other selves, an entity apart from other entities. The separation subprocess ordinarily begins at about 6 months postnatally. Prior to this phase, the infant is in the symbiotic phase (1–6 months), during which time the infant perceives and responds to the mother as if the two were fused or unseparated components of what Mahler termed a *dual unity*.

Fairbairn (1941) understood the symbiotic mother–infant relationship in terms of what he called *primary identification,* in accordance with which the infant perceives the mother as undifferentiated from himself. The mother–infant bond, which begins *in utero*, reaches its peak development during the symbiotic phase, thereafter becoming progressively attenuated during the ensuing *differentiation* (6–10 months), *practicing* (10–16 months), and *rapprochement* (16–26 months) *subphases of separation–individuation.* The mother–infant bond serves as prototype of all subsequent object relationships. Very early disturbances involving that bond, that is, infantile traumas during the first half year of life, yield two basic varieties of developmental pathology: bonding failure, producing psychoses of the autistic-presymbiotic type (Rinsley 1980a, 1982a), or so-called affectionless psychopaths (Horner 1979, Masterson 1981, Rinsley 1990).

It should be emphasized that the separation subprocess involves much more than the child's outward capacity to perceive himself as distinct from others. It also involves the gradual differentiation of the mental images or representations of oneself from those of others (Kernberg 1966, 1972, 1977). Critically associated with this differentiation of endopsychic or internalized images or representations is a profound transformation of the growing child's narcissism, such that his all good-all bad world view, based on the primitive pleasure principle and actuated by the pristine splitting mechanism, gradually gives way to an integrated good-and-bad (holistic) view based on the reality principle.

The shift from reliance on the pleasure principle toward expanding reliance on the reality principle represents one major component of the subprocess of *individuation*. Broadly defined, individuation encompasses all endopsychic transformations that promote the individual's development of increasingly effectual adaptation to internal and external (environmental) demands and requirements. It signifies the increasing effectiveness of ego functions (Federn 1952), including the internal and external ego boundaries, and those numerous perceptual and cognitive functions to which Hartmann (1939) has applied the term *ego apparatuses*, among which is the shift from recognitory memory toward evocative memory. From a cognitive standpoint, the child's individuation is reflected in the sequential development of stages of progressively mature thought (Piaget 1937), from sensorimotor through preoperational, concrete operational and, finally, fully (circular) operational ideation that reflects the capacity for abstraction and categorization (Goldstein's *abstract attitude* [1939, 1959]).

The key to an understanding of the separation–individuation process is found in the fact that both component subprocesses must necessarily run concurrently. In the healthily developing child, they are yoked together and proceed in accordance with the individual child's optimal and idiosyncratic developmental timetable. Where this is not the case, pathology ensues.

Chapter 5

Developmental Failure

Developmental failure or arrest, or lesser degrees of impairment conveyed by the term *deviation*, can be understood in terms of an inhibition of both sub-processes, or in terms of a dissociation or desynchronization of the one from the other. Both theory and clinical experience reveal that there are three permutations of developmental failure considered in these terms, only two of which are known:

1. Failure or arrest of *both* separation and individuation subprocesses.
2. Failure or arrest of separation with apparent preservation of individuation.
3. Failure or arrest of individuation with relative preservation of separation.

The clinical impairment resulting from the first permutation leads to psychosis or to the more primitively organized of the two major personality disorders, the borderline personality. That resulting from the second permutation leads to the less primitively organized of the two major personality disorders, the narcissistic personality. The developmental failure resulting from the third permutation, considered purely theoretically, cannot occur and has not been described.

FAILURE OF BOTH SEPARATION AND INDIVIDUATION

Failure or arrest of both subprocesses leads to sweeping impairments in the areas of selfhood, self–object differentiation, and in the sensing and testing of reality. The spectrum or continuum of these cases extends from autistic-presymbiotic psychoses (nuclear schizophrenia) through the major affective disorders and on to the borderline personality disorder (Rinsley 1982a).

A concept of the pathogenesis of the borderline personality was formulated (Masterson and Rinsley 1975) based on the contributions of Mahler and her colleagues (Mahler 1971, Mahler et al. 1975). Following Mahler's (1971) lead, the origin of borderline character pathology was traced to developmental arrest occurring no later than the rapprochement subphase of separation–individuation. It is during this subphase that the toddler makes his most determined early developmental effort toward self-object differentiation, hence toward generating a significant awareness of his selfhood as distinct from that of others. It is also during this period that the child develops object permanency and, as a consequence, lays the foundation for his evolving ability to fantasize. In turn, the child's expanding use of fantasy accompanies and catalyzes the inception of preoperational thought (Piaget 1937), which underlies the child's potential for the development of his capacity for foreplanning.

Of inestimable importance as a consequence of the child's working-through of the events of the rapprochement subphase is the development of the capacity to mourn, resulting from the child's working-through of the depressive position (Klein 1935, 1940), which normally begins in earnest during this subphase. The child's working-through of the depressive position induces a number of other interrelated accomplishments that are indispensable for further healthy development. These include (1) the shift from part-object relations to whole-object relations, (2) the inception of normal repression, and (3) the establishment of "sphincter specificity" (Kut Rosenfeld and Sprince 1963), as a result of which the child's polymorphous-perverse eroticism begins to give way to a consolidation of his or her sexual identity in conformity with anatomical gender.

As Melanie Klein (1945) pointed out, the child's successful negotiation of the oedipal phase is based on the accomplishment of the work of the depressive position; thus, for the child, the parents assume the character of whole objects. The momentous effect of this discovery was to replace Freud's Oedipus complex by the depressive position as fundamental to psychopathogenesis generally and to affirm depression, however clinically expressed, as a major feature of all forms of psychopathology, including borderline and narcissistic personality disorders, in which "abandonment depression" plays a decisive pathogenetic role. Based on intensive work with borderline preadolescents, adolescents, adults, and their dysfunctional families, the depersonifying mother–child relationship that underlies the failure of these interrelated maturational processes in the borderline personality was discovered (Masterson and Rinsley 1975). The maternal message at the core of that relationship was that any effort by the child to desymbiotize, to grow apart or away from the mother, to separate, would be met with a withdrawal of maternal nurturance; conversely, to remain symbiotic—hence passive, ineffectual, and ultimately self-defeating—would guarantee an ongoing supply of such nurturance. Put succinctly, this message amounted to "Without me (mother) you cannot exist!"—the "Don't Be (Without Me)" command of transactional analysis. For the child enmeshed in such a relationship, growth and development come to signify disaster and success signifies failure. The developmental arrest that typifies the borderline personality thus finds the victim at a position between Stages 2 and 3 of Kernberg's (1972) schema of internalized object relations (see Chapter 15, p. 93).

FAILURE OR ARREST OF SEPARATION WITH
APPARENT PRESERVATION OF INDIVIDUATION

In contrast to the pathogenesis of the borderline person-ality, that of the (higher-level) narcissistic personality is a consequence of a disarticulation of these two subprocesses (Rinsley 1980b, 1984, 1985). As Kulish (1988) has shown, such a disarticulation was postulated by Freud (1913a) as underlying the pathogenesis of the obsessional neurosis, conceived in terms of a chronological outstripping of libid-inal development by ego development or the development of ego in excess of the development of drive (A. Freud 1966). In a classic paper devoted to precocious ego develop-ment (the pseudo-mature child), Speers and Morter (1980) described the pathological results of such a disarticulation in the cases of three adultomorphized children:

1. Incomplete object constancy, self constancy, and phallic dominance, the last of these signifying im-paired sphincter specificity or stabilization.
2. Persistent good–bad splitting.
3. Separation anxiety defended against by means of fantasies of omnipotence, resulting in a highly vul-nerable sense of self.
4. Avoidance of the prospect of separation and accom-panying overwhelming feelings of helplessness through maintenance of constant contact with the mother through verbal "fascination" and the ex-pressed need for endless approbative mirroring. These children's mothers discouraged regression and

insisted on "grown-up" behavior. Pleasing and being admired by the mother were the order of the day and required a facade of nonangry, competent behavior.

The core pathogenic maternal message in these cases was that the child could go through the motions of separation from the mother, could appear to grow up and apart from her, but only if everything so accomplished was in relation to her (Rinsley 1984, 1985). Thus, cognitive-intellectual achievement was stimulated and rewarded within a persistently symbiotic context. This variety of pathogenic mother–child relationship, with its emphasis on cognitive growth without genuine empathic attunement between its protagonists, results in the precocious evolution in the child of defenses centering on isolation of affect, including intellectualization and various forms of guilt-laden, ritualistic undoing. These are the hallmarks of the obsessional personality, behaviorally combining emotional coldness and aloofness toward, and an inability to generate meaningful, empathic relationships with individuals other than the mother.

Chapter 6

Maternal Characteristics

The pivotal role of the mother in the pathogenesis of borderline or narcissistic personality in her child cannot be adequately appreciated without reference to the child's father in the case of two-parent families, or to his absence in the case of the one-parent family. Abelin's (1971a,b, 1975, 1980) studies clearly indicate the father's significance for the child *ab initio* and during the symbiotic phase and the ensuing differentiation and practicing subphases of separation–individuation. Especially significant is the father's role, which peaks during the rapprochement subphase, in promoting the child's desymbiotization through the process of disidentification with the mother (in the case of the male child) and in serving as a healthy oedipal object (in the case of the female child); both of these processes reinforce the child's early steps toward the consolidation of the child's gender identity.

Of inestimable importance is the father's role as spousal nurturer of the mother, both genitally and generally, which in turn reinforces the mother's capacity to nurture the child and to promote the child's healthy separation from her. The mother's "good enough" function vis-à-vis her youngster (Winnicott 1950–1955) is thus optimized through the presence of a "good enough" spouse who is attuned to her needs and who provides her with essential assistance in the coparenting process.

Extensive clinical experience with the mothers of borderline preadults and adults revealed an almost stereotypical pattern of their early interaction with their children.

They took pride in and found significant gratification from their infants' dependency . . . from birth through the second postnatal month. Beginning with the differentiation subphase . . . however, their responses to their developing infant took on a predictable pattern, i.e., they in various ways reinforced the infant's passivity by "rewarding" the latter's passive-dependent clinging behavior and, again in various ways, withdrew from or actively "punished" the infant whenever the infant displayed more actively aggressive, exploratory . . . activity. Typically, the . . . mother exuded happy satisfaction when asked about her experiences with her neonate, only to lapse into frowning, emotional blandness, or disdain when discussing her progressively more active infant during the latter half of the first postnatal year and beyond.

These mothers were recapitulating with their children the separation–individuation difficulties they had themselves experienced with their own mothers. They were, in fact, engaged in extended, pathological mutual clinging with their children in order to ward off the everpresent, underlying abandonment depression associated with their own failure to have successfully negotiated the separation–individuation phase. The husbands or consorts of these mothers, the progenitors of the latters' future borderline children and adults, fitted a reasonably stereotyped pattern as well. They were either absent from the beginning or had absconded from the family during the child's pre-school years, or else proved to be non-nurturant males with an above-average incidence of spouse and child abuse and neglect, alcohol and substance abuse, and antisociality. The mothers' choice of these weak and defective spousal partners reflected their need to recapitulate the defective relationships they had had with their own fathers. As expected, these "marriages" also reflected powerful underlying incestuous issues contaminating the spousal and parent–child relationships.

The mothers of future narcissistic personalities, while yet harboring the abandonment–separation–depression conflicts common to the mothers of the future borderline personalities, were generally better organized psychologically. Speers and Morter's (1980) description accords well with my own observations of these mothers' interactions with their children, especially during the rapprochement subphase.

> The mother–child interaction "discouraged regression and insisted that 'grown-up' behavior prevail. Words replaced physical contact; thus, an insistence that precociously mature modalities of interaction take precedence over the primitive modalities of touch, smell, taste, and near vision. There was a demand that . . . separation and the concomitant anxieties be coped with by words and activities which were pleasing to mother. . . . The message from the mother was consistently one of 'You are a big boy/girl now.' These children were not permitted (nor do they permit themselves) to feel and express the rage of separation, the humiliation of helplessness, nor the loss of omnipotence with an available, empathic mother. Thus, being pleasing to and being admired by the mother became essential and required a facade of nonangry, competent behavior." [Speers and Morter 1980, pp. 460–461]

As might be expected, these families presented a picture of lesser degrees of gross or overt dysfunctionality when compared to the families of future borderline children and adults. More of them were biparental, with a high degree of skew toward the adultomorphizing maternal figure and a weak paternal figure who had, in effect, relinquished executive and parental control to her. In many such families, it appeared as if the father's sole role was that of stud, with little, ineffectual, or no sustained interest in parenting once the issue had arrived. Here again, investigation revealed that the marital pattern was recapitulating a pattern common to the mother's own infamily, in which the female child, adultomorphically extruded from the nest, proceeded to extrude her own child in the next generation. The defensive omnipotence of the narcissistic child (Bleiberg 1987, 1988a,b) could readily be noted to reflect, in part, the omnipotence of the dominating mother within the family.

Thus, in contrast to the mother of the future borderline personality, who must threaten her child's very existence should the youngster attempt to separate from her, the mother of the future narcissistic personality presents her child with a paradox: achievement, while encouraged, must be based upon the child's failure to separate from her. How, indeed, does this come to pass?

The answer is found in the discovery that the mother's adultomorphization of her child results from her over-determined need to perceive the child as a depersonified quasi-parent figure (Rinsley 1971, 1980c, 1985, Rinsley and Hall 1962). Thus, she must cling to the child in accordance with two paradoxical (doubly binding) modes of inter-action:

1. She must cling to the child, through the child's achievements, in order to maintain a flow of spurious parental nurturance from him, therewith to bolster her own deficient sense of self-esteem.
2. She must prematurely extrude the child from her, to disavow the child's dependence on her, in order to disavow her own unmet dependency needs. Thus, the child's spurious adulthood comes to reflect her own spurious adulthood as a consequence of pathological projective identification.

Chapter 7

Psychostructural and Adaptive Effects

Kernberg's (1977) penetrating study of the endopsychic and adaptive consequences of the borderline personality's developmental impairment led him to formulate the structural characteristics of the borderline personality organization (adapted):

Specific Structural Characteristics
Identity diffusion (impaired ego integration)
Primitive defenses based on splitting

Splitting *per se*
Primitive idealization and devaluation
Projective identification
Denial and omnipotence
Nonspecific Structural Characteristics
Ego weakness
Impaired anxiety tolerance and impulse control
Lack of developed sublimatory channels
Impaired superego integration
Genetic-dynamic characteristics
Undue contamination of oedipal issues with
aggression
Exaggerated idealization of heterosexual and
homosexual love objects
Intermingling of parental images projected
onto the therapist
Genital strivings contaminated by pre-oedipal
strivings
Premature oedipalization of pre-oedipal issues

Adler (1985) characterized the central problem of the borderline personality as a failure to have developed a "holding-soothing introject" as a consequence of severely impaired evocative memory. Modell (1968, 1984) considered that the borderline individual's impaired object relationships result from the pathological persistence of transitional object relatedness; that is, the borderline individual's relations with others reflect the basic features of the infant's use of the transitional object (Winnicott 1951). Of course, transitional object relatedness, a variety of part–

object relatedness, reflects the individual's failure to have worked through the depressive position.

The future borderline child, subjected to the doubly binding maternal message of reward for passivity and incompetence and withdrawal or rejection (abandonment) for growth (Masterson and Rinsley 1975), proceeds to internalize both components of the message, thereby generating the *split object relations unit of the borderline* (Table 7–1).

Credit must be accorded to Fairbairn (1944), who initially described the two split-off part–object representations, as noted above, as what he terms the *split internalized bad object*, the sundered internal image of the ungratifying maternal breast. Fairbairn further considered that the internalization of this split "dynamic object" induced in the child a concomitant splitting of the child's ego, the resulting products of which came into relationship with the split-off components of this object. Employing Fairbairn's terminology, his account of what turned out to be the Masterson-Rinsley split object relations unit of the borderline may be seen in Table 7–2, (Rinsley 1979, 1982c) on p. 35.

Although that rendition of Fairbairn's endopsychic structures is oversimplified for the purposes of this presentation, it may be noted that the withdrawing or rejecting component of the split object relations unit is analogous to Fairbairn's R.O.-Anti-L.E., whereas the rewarding component is analogous to his E.O.-L.E.

The pathologically persistent "all good-all bad" world view that typifies the borderline personality can be traced to the presence and functioning of these split internalized

Table 7-1.

Structure of the split object relations unit of the borderline.

Component	Part-object representation	Linking affect	Part-self representation
Withdrawing or rejecting	A maternal image that is hostile, critical, attacking, withdrawing of supplies and support in the face of the child's assertiveness or other efforts toward separation–individuation	Chronic anger and frustration, feeling thwarted and incompetent, which cover profound underlying abandonment depression	A self-image of being "bad," helpless, incompetent, ugly, empty, guilty, defective, etc.

/\/ SPLIT /\/

Rewarding	A maternal image offering approval, support, and supplies for regressive, clinging behavior	Feeling "good," being fed, gratification of the wish for (symbiotic) reunion	A self-image of being the "good," passive, compliant child

34

Table 7–2.
Fairbairn's rendering of the split object relations unit.

Object		Ego

Rejecting (R.O.)
    A maternal image that
        is hostile, withholding,
        and attacking
	LINKED	Antilibidinal (Anti-L.E.)
		    A self-image that is
		        hostile, self-deprecatory,
		        and self-defeating

/\/\/\/\/\/\/\/\/\/\/\/\/ SPLIT \/\/\/\/\/\/\/\/\/\/\/\/\/\		

Exciting (E.O.)
    A maternal image that
        is alluring, exciting,
        seductive, promising
        immediate pleasure
        and gratification
	LINKED	Libidinal (L.E.)
		    A self-image that is
		        excitable, impulsive,
		        demanding, feeling entitled
		        to immediate pleasure and
		        gratification

structures (Kernberg 1972, 1977). The "all good" valence stems from the effects of the rewarding component of the split object relations unit, analogous to Fairbairn's E.O.-L.E., whereas the "all bad" valence stems from the withdrawing or rejecting component, analogous to Fairbairn's R.O.-Anti-L.E. The functioning of these split structures underlies the borderline personality's daunting ego weakness, with ensuing internal dysregulation, object impermanency, and unstabilized cognition, affect, and behavior. They constitute the unstable archaic selfobjects that Kohut has described.

The narcissistic personality shares the foregoing psychostructural and adaptive disabilities with the borderline personality, including the latter's underlying abandonment depression, although their symptomatic expression is less evident in terms of proneness to regression and grossly disruptive (acting out) behavior.

Kohut views the pathology of the narcissistic personality as the result of a weakened or impaired self, the tenuous cohesiveness of which is maintained by means of an overweening need for approbative mirroring by others (Kohut 1971, 1977, Kohut and Wolf 1978). According to this view, the narcissistic personality's unseparated condition is maintained by means of the persistence of developmentally primitive selfobject relationships; these are characterized by the persistence of the young child's *grandiose self* (omnipotence) and *idealized parental image* (pathological idealization of others, leading to reactive devaluation of them when the idealizing needs are unmet). The cause of this state of psychological affairs is to be found in the parents', especially the mother's, failure to empathically mirror the growing child's grandiose and idealizing needs. Kohut's concept of parental mirroring is akin to Mahler's concept of mutual cueing or communicative matching between mother and child, which is critically important for the child's optimal development, particularly throughout the separation–individuation phase. It is also akin to Bion's (1967) concept of the maternal container.

Complementary to these concepts is Kernberg's (1970) view that the narcissistic personality's representational world is governed by a fusion of what he terms the *ideal self, ideal object,* and *real self,* which results in the devaluation and destruction of object-images. The narcissistic personality identifies himself with his ideal(ized) self-images in order to deny his dependency on external objects as well as on the inner images of those objects. Associated with this is a denial of the unacceptable aspects of his self-image, which are in turn projected into external objects, thereby reinforcing their devaluation. The symptomatic expressions of these phenomena include intense envy, interpersonal aloofness, overt grandiosity covering deep-seated feelings of inferiority and worthlessness, and chronic boredom and dissatisfaction (Akhtar and Thomson 1982, Rinsley 1989).

The internalized object relations of the narcissistic personality, considered in terms of the split object relations unit, have not been as thoroughly explored and understood as have those of the borderline personality. As noted, however, both personalities share the underlying abandonment depression: the borderline personality whenever a step toward growth (= emancipation) beckons, the narcissistic personality whenever the prospect of a meaningful relationship makes an appearance, thereby threatening the powerful maternal introject, and when the environment fails to meet his demands for approbative mirroring. It is very likely that the elements of the split object relations unit of the borderline are also operative in the case of the narcissistic personality, albeit in a less discombobulating fashion. Accordingly, Kohut's (1977) term *stable archaic selfobjects* may be applied to them.

In the case of both personalities, the failure of maternal empathy, of interpersonal attunement, which Kohut has emphasized as fundamental to the development of the narcissistic personality, assumes polar opposite forms. Rather than being promised reward for clinging dependency, as in the case of the borderline-to-be child, the narcissist-to-be child is promised reward if he "gets up and gets out" during the years when he most needs to indulge his otherwise healthy dependency needs. In this case, what is egregiously evident is the failure of maternal empathic attunement to the child's interdigitated needs for expanding competency *and* dependency, for grandiose and idealizing mirroring, hence for his overall need to be perceived and dealt with as the child that he is.

Analysis of cases of validly diagnosed narcissistic personality in children, adolescents, and adults has led to a mixed model view of their internalized object relations (Greenberg and Mitchell 1983). The child's internalization of the adultomorphizing mother leads to the establishment of a powerful, persecutory superego introject that demands perfectionistic accomplishment in relation to itself, hence at the expense of other object relationships. Over time, a powerfully persecutory and castrating paternal component fuses with this introject, which symbolizes the child's need to identify with a father figure by means of the generation of a distorted representation of otherwise healthy male aggressiveness and executive competence. The child's ego, driven by this introject, experiences encapsulated rage, hence depression as it quails in the face of the superego's demands and the preclusion of other object relationships that result from them.

The *solution* that the ego adopts under such drastic circumstances is to identify with this sadistic superego (Freud 1917, Rado 1928), with the resulting development of manic defenses (Klein 1935, 1940). As described by Kernberg (1980), these include:

1. *Identification with the superego,* leading to a denial of depressive guilt and aggression, which are then projected into others, who come to be depreciated and hated.
2. *Manic triumph,* reflecting the ego's death wishes to-

ward the introjected superego object, expressed in feelings of:

- *Omnipotence*, in which there occurs a denial of one's vulnerability and one's need to be dependent on others, expressed in
- *Contempt* for others, and
- *Idealization*, used to ward off the dangerousness of others and one's dependency on them.

It is now possible to present a more thoroughgoing picture of the dynamic psychopathology of the narcissistic personality. The adaptational profile of this personality type combines the operation of obsessional (affect-isolative) defenses and episodically triumphant manic-like experiences, both derived from the impress of the superego introject. Underlying these is the everpresent, pre-eruptive abandonment depression, which is in actuality a variety of dysphoric separation anxiety. In turn, this depressive dysphoria further combines with the depression resulting from the superego's periodic assaults on the ego, both of which underlie the clinical (characterological) depression that is universal among narcissistic personalities. As a result, these patients present with complaints of chronic (depressive) boredom and ennui or with a clinical picture of generally muted, atypical bipolar symptomatology within a setting of longstanding emotional coldness and aloofness resulting from the operation of the obsessional defenses.

Finally, in contrast to the borderline personality, who suffers from severely impaired object permanency (evocative memory), the narcissistic personality maintains an intact capacity to summon up inner images of others in their absence. However, there is a significant impairment of (libidinal) object constancy (A. Freud 1960, 1968, Fraiberg 1969) such that the evoked images are either insufficiently drive-reducing (tension-easing), or actually induce various mixtures of anxiety and depression (abandonment depression) *unless the images are perceived as more or less direct representations of the superego introject.* Indeed, for the narcissistic personality, not only are relationships other than with the adultomorphizing maternal introject forbidden in the external world, but they are forbidden in the internal world as well, hence their failure to contribute to ongoing psychostructural growth and development.

From a theoretical standpoint, the foregoing formulations concerning these two personality types will be noted to represent a "mixed model" approach to the understanding of their development and symptomatology (Greenberg and Mitchell 1983). Thus, although a predominant emphasis is placed on object-relations concepts (e.g., Fairbairn's dynamic structures), it is also necessary to invoke more classical concepts of endopsychic structure and function (e.g., ego and super-ego), especially in applying to our task the enormously important insights provided by the contributions of Melanie Klein.

Chapter 8

The Centrality of Pre-oedipal Trauma

In her masterful biography of Melanie Klein, Phyllis Grosskurth (1987) condenses much of the essence of Klein's path-blazing contributions as follows: "Quite clearly the depressive position has replaced the Oedipus complex as the central problem to be surmounted in development" (p. 217). The inestimable importance of the growing child's ability to work through, hence to healthily transit the depressive position, lies in the fact that the child must necessarily mourn the separation from the mother; this means that he must proceed to extricate himself from the mother–infant symbiosis in order to emerge as a freestanding personage capable of genuine intimacy.

The depth of Melanie Klein's insights into the interrelated processes of the working through of the depressive position and the achievement of separation (or rather, separation–individuation) is awesome indeed. In accordance with them, the Oedipus complex, which classical psychoanalysis has traditionally regarded as the key to an understanding of both normal and pathological psychological development, assumes a derivative or secondary position. Thus, from a clinical standpoint, where oedipal conflicts loom large in the range of psychopathological syndromes, as they invariably do, one must explore more deeply into antecedent (pre-oedipal) traumas and resulting developmental conflicts if therapeutic success is to be achieved. Fairbairn (1944) put this succinctly when he wrote that "a sufficiently deep analysis of the Oedipus situation invariably reveals that [it] is built up around the figures of an internal exciting mother and an internal rejecting mother" (p. 124). As noted, these two maternal figures comprise Fairbairn's split internalized bad object (the E.O. and the R.O., respectively), affiliated with which, from the side of the child, are the L.E. and the Anti-L.E., respectively.

Considered in terms of Kohut's self psychology, the issues and conflicts associated with a developed Oedipus complex are to be understood as manifestations of breakdown or fragmentation of the self, and are not in themselves manifestations of normal or healthy psychological development, a consideration with which Fairbairn's view is in basic agreement. It follows that, while oedipal-type conflicts and rivalries certainly appear during the latter part of the child's pre-school years, the healthy child, possessed of a sound, nascent self-identity resulting from an optimal balance of interdigitated growth and dependency needs, proceeds to deal with these conflicts and rivalries with little or no personal and interpersonal perturbation. Of course, such balance is achieved as a result of the child's mutual attunement with an empathic, good enough mother and a healthy father who both nurtures the mother and provides for the child's ongoing separation–individuation.

The same may be said of the period of adolescence, the regressive-recapitulative features of which were classically cited to support the long since discredited view of the adolescent as a turmoil-ridden, even normally psychotic victim of untrammeled instinctual drives unleashed by surging and shifting hormones and the psychological effects of frightening bodily changes. Quite the contrary. As Masterson (1967, 1972) long ago pointed out, the turmoil-ridden adolescent is not healthy, and as Offer also long ago pointed out (Offer 1967, Offer et al. 1965), the healthy adolescent is not turmoil-ridden.

PART II

TREATMENT

Axios ópheleîn toùs àlgoûntas.
    —Motto of Alpha Omega Alpha

Chapter 9

Acting Out

A goodly portion of the borderline personality's symptomatology finds expression in behavior, a characterologic feature that often renders the borderline individual perplexing, irritating, and disruptive to others, and poses difficult and not rarely insuperable difficulties for those who would treat him. While generally less wildly disruptive than the borderline personality, the overt attitudes and behavior of his higher-level congener, the narcissistic personality, are fully capable of undoing the analyst's or therapist's efforts. Accordingly, this discussion will begin with a brief consideration of the concept and phenomenon of acting out as revelant to the psychoanalytic treatment of both personalities, especially during its early or opening phase.

As originally defined by Freud (1905, 1914b), acting out referred to the tendency of some analysands to express inner conflicts in behavior rather than in words within the analytic situation. As noted by Aldrich (1987), the term has since come to define any actions with an antisocial bias (Rexford 1978) and all kinds of impulsive, pathological, antisocial, and dangerous behavior (Bernstein and Walker 1981). Ferenczi (1919) defined acting out more inclusively with the term *alloplastic*, meaning an organism's adaptation by altering its environment, in contrast to *autoplastic*, meaning adaptation by altering itself. The term *acting in* has come into more limited general usage to apply to Freud's original definition of acting out. Bernstein and Walker (1981) further distinguish between behavior that expresses unconscious conflict, which they term acting out, and behavior that results primarily from impaired impulse control, which they term *acting up*. In the following discussion, *acting out* will be employed in the more extended sense of Ferenczi's term *alloplastic*.

Although acting out serves as a form of experimental recollection, especially among younger children and adolescents (Ekstein and Friedman 1957), its most generally accepted function is as a defense *against* remembering (Fenichel 1945), that is, acting out serves the purposes of repression. Insofar as repression in these cases is less than optimally developed, as it bears all the earmarks of splitting (Fairbairn 1954), it may be said that acting out subserves the splitting defense. One notes this evident fact in cases involving substance abuse, sexual perversion, and antisocial behavior in specific, and in general in the personality-disordered individual's propensity to engage in self-defeating and self-destructive forms of behavior (Freud 1916). Such behavior may be considered as a variety of self-intoxication (*selbstgiftig*); hence, as soon as feasible in treatment, the patient will require what can best be considered to be detoxification (Rinsley 1988a).

In cases of substance abuse, detoxification consists in the interdiction of the use of the toxic substance. By the same token, the personality-disordered patient's toxic behavior must necessarily be interrupted and brought to a halt if expressive treatment is to continue with any prospect of a favorable outcome. Put more simply, such treatment cannot be effectively carried out with an alcoholic who continues to drink, with a sexual pervert who continues to engage in perverse sexual acts, or with a thief while he continues to steal. In such cases, interdiction amounts to outside intervention or, in more technical terms, the imposition of external controls, applied as needed in order to bring the toxic behavior to a halt.

The basis for the application of such controls may be understood in terms of the necessity to begin to put to rest the pathologically persistent underlying affectomotor lability or instability that is responsible for the patient's alloplasticity, based in turn on the patient's failure to have developed a serviceable holding-soothing introject (Adler 1985). The alloplastic (acting-out) behavior may thus be seen as an expression of failure of internal self-regulation — in classical terms, of failure of the ego's self-monitoring and self-regulating function. The imposition of (external) regulatory controls is necessary, therefore, to allow the therapist to serve as an interim auxiliary ego to begin to reduce and modulate the patient's condition of internal dysregulation. As this successfully occurs, the defensive barrier against remembering proceeds to lift, thereby facilitating the patient's accessibility to therapeutic confrontation, clarification, and interpretation.*

One cannot easily miss the analogy of this early therapeutic maneuvering with personality-disordered patients to the proper disciplining of otherwise healthy young children. Like the older borderline patient, for example, the young child lacks a full complement of inner controls for impulsive, dysregulated behavior, hence requires the sensitive, disciplined imposition of such controls to facilitate their internalization based on identification with the control-givers. By the same token, the aim of imposing external controls in the case of the personality-disordered patient is to facilitate the patient's early-on identification with the protectively disciplining function of the therapist or analyst, an essential early step toward the eventual formation of a therapeutic alliance.

This early step in treatment symbolically recapitulates basic features of the early parent–child relationship centering on Kohut's grandiose self and idealized parental

---

*Although there is reason to question Fairbairn's (1954) view of repression and splitting as one and the same process (Rinsley 1988c), clinical experience attests to their closely combined functioning in these cases, the most evident examples of which are patients with multiple personality disorder (Braun 1984, Clary 1984).

image. The child's existential dilemma, as it were, concerns his infantile grandiosity within a context of adaptive immaturity. The child begins to deal with this dilemma by projecting his grandiosity into the parent, whom he therewith proceeds to idealize. In turn, this idealization catalyzes the child's internalization of the parent's competency. This ongoing, to-and-fro, projective–introjective process involving parent and child constitutes what Bion (1967) termed the container-contained function, which forms the basis for the child's beginning build-up of his nascent identity. Put another way, the child grandiosely displays his as yet immature competencies to the parent, and the latter receives them, mirrors them, and having remodeled them, reprojects the resulting products into the child. During these complex maturational interactions, the child must at times attempt to scotomatize, eliminate, or vanquish the parent, rendered into a powerful, persecutory object in the child's view as a consequence of the child's grandiose projections.

Although aspects of these pristine parent–child interactions animate analytic therapeutic processes generally, they become much more evident in the treatment of borderline and narcissistic personalities. Their particular significance during the early stages of treatment relates to the patient's ability to begin to internalize external controls that the therapist finds necessary to impose (Voth 1972). Like the young child, the personality-disordered patient poignantly experiences frustration and anger when the therapist fails to mirror his projected grandiosity by failing to take charge early in the course of treatment, and much of the patient's early-on acting out serves to test the therapist's willingness and ability to do so as an indicator of the therapist's basic trustworthiness.

> Oftentimes, the therapist's failure to "take charge" provokes an outburst of statements and nonverbal behavior by the patient that signify the need to devalue the therapist. Despite the fact that the patient must necessarily resist the imposition of control, his resistance amounts to the "message" to the therapist, "I'm angry at you for failing to protect me from myself—you're supposed to be all-powerful and you just proved that you aren't!" Such behavior by the patient is frequently puzzling and confusing to the therapist until its origin is understood.

The fact is that the patient, like the young child, is more than slightly aware of his incompetence, expressed in part in varieties of self-defeating and self-destructive acting out, including the negative therapeutic reaction (Danielian and Lister 1988). Accordingly, the therapist's failure or unwillingness to impose controls conveys an inability to provide protective safety, to say "No!" when urgently needed to curb the patient's acting out. As a consequence, the patient perceives the therapist as an impotent, incompetent parental figure, an aloof, detached personage who is empathically insensitive to his needs. What is more, the patient's pathologically persistent infantile grandiosity causes him to blame himself for the therapist's incompetence, as expressed in the latter's avoidant-appearing aloofness. The result is a resurgence of primitive guilt, resulting in turn in fresh rounds of self-defeating and self-injurious behavior of an expiatory nature.

The more comprehensive "message" which the patient conveys in such a behavioral sequence may be noted as follows: "I projected my grandiosity into you and made you all-wonderful and all-powerful. But I also projected my helplessness into you and made you incompetent. Thus, you failed to protect me and I am enraged at you and guilty for what I have done to rob you of your power, and now I must hurt myself to atone for the guilt I feel over what I have done to you and stolen from you!" Inherent in this sadomasochistic stance are the dynamics of primitive envy and greed (Klein 1957, 1963).

Chapter 10

Dealing with Idealization and Devaluation

Idealization (primitive idealization) and devaluation are defensive operations, related to splitting, which are components of Kernberg's (1977) specific structural characteristics of the borderline personality. They appear early in the therapy of borderline and narcissistic personalities, and the manner by which the therapist or analyst deals with them determines the difference between the two different approaches to them: Kernberg (1975, 1982a,b) and Kohut and the self psychologists (Adler 1985, Hedges 1983, Kohut 1977, Kohut and Wolf 1978). Kernberg generally assumes that idealization and devaluation represent resistances that convey the patient's need to split the therapist, as it were, into all-good and all-bad objects as an expression of the splitting of good and bad self- and object-representations within himself. By so doing, the patient, among other things, attempts to scotomatize the therapist as a whole object (good + bad), thereby to avoid the work of the depressive position (Klein 1935, 1940, 1946).

Although both Kernberg and Kohut acknowledge the etiological role of a defective self in pathological narcissism, including its manifestation as idealization and devaluation within the therapeutic or analytic process (Teicholz 1978), self psychology holds that their early appearance within the therapeutic transference should not be considered, confronted, or interpreted as resistances as such (Kohut 1971, 1977). According to this view, the patient would experience such actions by the therapist as reflecting the therapist's unconscious need to inhibit or preclude the patient's need for reflective mirroring, hence for the therapist's acknowledgment and affirmation of the patient's needy infantile self. Thus, the therapist's confrontations could be seen to reflect the powerful countertransferential need to disavow the patient's need for narcissistic mirroring in order to avoid recognizing his own need for it, as this is reawakened as a consequence of the patient's transference-derived projections (Kohut 1971).

From both technical and empathic standpoints, a judicious combination of both approaches is optimal. Obviously, none of us, therapist or not, can easily withstand being scourged by others, including our patients, which threatens to reawaken in us our primal terror of abandonment. Nor can we blithely abide in our patients' bouts of idealizing love for us, given the constraints of ethics and the fact that they threaten to reawaken in us our equally terrifying fear of regressive engulfment. Thus, one best deals with the patient's primitive idealizing and devaluing maneuvers by knowing how to draw the patient's attention to their undeniable resistance meaning, while at the same time not retreating from the requirement that they be approbatively mirrored.

An example of this dual approach may be illustrated in the case of an exceptionally attractive, intellectually superior, divorced 26-year-old woman who, in the course of an early therapeutic hour, experienced sexual feelings for the therapist to such a degree that she suddenly jumped up, flung her arms around him, and began kissing him on the cheek. Momentarily taken aback by this sudden turn of events, the therapist quickly regained his composure, very gently disengaged himself from the patient, and guided her to a chair across from his desk. The following dialogue ensued:

P (crying softly): "I'm terribly sorry doctor, but I just couldn't help myself—I don't know what came over me!"

T: "Mrs. G., I'm complimented that you have positive feelings for me. Of course, as we both know, ethics would forbid my returning them in kind. Nevertheless, Mrs. G., positive feelings can serve the purposes of our work together. They are welcome without any attempt on my part to exploit them."

P: "I know that. I'm sorry and I feel ashamed of myself."

T: "You haven't lost face, Mrs. G. Let's take a look at what happened and try to understand it."

There ensued an illuminating account, by the patient, of how her parents, particularly her cold, aloof father, had never praised her for her beauty and her superior literary talent and of how her former husband of three years had devalued her and attempted to press her into service as his slavish maidservant.

P: "After only a few months I began to feel like his slave. He turned out to be cold and unfeeling, our sex was just for his satisfaction, and I began to hate him!"

T: "Might that have some connection with what just happened here?"

P: "Hmm—do you think that maybe I was trying to put you in the same position as F. (*the ex-husband*)?"

T: "What do *you* think?"

P: "Well, it could be true—yes, I think so! But I think I was also trying to get something from you, maybe some positive feelings, and I'm glad you didn't push me away and make me feel even worse than I do."

T: "Who was it you wanted to get those feelings from in the first place?"

P: "I'm sure it was my father! Hmm—is what I just did what you call a father transference?"

T: "What do you think?"

P: "Hmm, yes, I think so! So I wanted you to love me but I expected you to push me away like he did. That's the story of my life with men!"

There followed an account of the patient's ungratifying experiences in several premarital affairs with what proved to be narcissistic, exploitative men, culminating in her marriage to such a man.

T: "Let's look at how all those made you feel."

P: "I can tell you! I felt rotten and I felt enraged! I wanted to get back at them!"

T: "To prove what?"

P: "To prove they were nothing but bums!"

T: "What about what happened here a few minutes ago?"

P: "Hmm—maybe I wanted to prove that you were another one just like them."

Several ensuing hours came to be devoted to an exploration of how the patient felt ultimately responsible for her plight, that she must have been a "bad person" to have warded off closeness to her parents, her paramours, and her husband. The process then turned to an exploration of what proved to be her blighted and failed mother–daughter relationship, to the deeper origins of her failed maternal identification, and her resultant inability to experience herself as a "real woman" worthy and capable of genuine and loving intimacy with a "real man."

Of course, idealization and devaluation are often used by the patient to negate the detoxification process. The following case excerpt illustrates how the therapist's imposition of verbal controls very quickly resulted in the uncovering of highly significant material during the second hour in the pretreatment evaluative phase of analytic treatment:

The prospective patient was an unmarried professional woman in her late thirties with a prior diagnosis of narcissistic personality disorder with hysteriform features. During the initial evaluative session, she revealed that she frequently engaged in bar-hopping. During these excursions, she often took the men home and had intercourse with them, and on a few occasions, she managed to acquire a sadistic partner who inflicted various minor injuries on her. When told that she must totally desist from any such activity as well as from sexual relations under any circumstances to be accepted for treatment, the following interaction ensued:

P: "Well, you're really high and mighty! Who are you to tell me I can't have sex if I want to?"

T: "What I'm telling you is that I won't accept you for treatment if you do."

P: "Well, I suppose I could fool you and you'd never know."

T: "As you well know, Miss J., you'd really be fooling yourself. And besides, I'm sure that the truth would eventually come out."

P: "Well, I suppose you're right."

In this case, the patient's devaluing expostulations served the initial purpose of deflecting her and the prospective therapist's attention away from her toxic, self-endangering acting out, an overdetermined pattern that subsequent analysis revealed to serve other purposes akin to those in the case of the previously reported patient. Her "high and mighty" remark could be seen to reflect her underlying idealizing need. In the following (second) hour, the patient began by reporting a most revealing transference dream:

P: "I was in Las Vegas in a casino with hundreds of people in the audience, watching a hilarious stand-up comic. I was in the first row, right underneath him on the stage, looking up at him. We were all rolling in the aisles, he was so funny. Then, as I was watching him, he turned into my father and I felt a little uneasy in the dream. Then, when he finished up his act, he whipped out his penis and peed into my open mouth and I woke up in a sweat."

Analysis of this dream constituted part of the analytic work that was accomplished during the first eight months following the inception of the therapeutic process. Among many other findings brought out by the dream analysis, one of them confirmed the initial impression that the dream had occurred as a consequence of the therapist's imposition of verbal controls during the initial evaluative hour with the patient. It had to do with the patient's view of her father, hence of all men, as misusers and exploiters of women. The manifest dream content in which the patient's father, an "as-if, comical buffoon," urinated into her open mouth conveyed a condensed symbolism of her view of sexual intercourse as the man urinating into (contaminating) the woman's vagina and of the father, and men generally, as de-valued objects ("buffoons"). The patient's failed sphincter speci-ficity was reflected in a cloaca-like phantasy according to which the male ejaculatory product (semen) was equated with urine and the vagina became a mouth. The early transference meaning of the dream was evident: the prospective therapist, a man, became the devalued and devaluing paternal figure whom the patient could "fool" by concealing her sexual exploits, and who in the end would prove himself to be another exploiter and con-taminator. A much deeper meaning, arrived at in the later stages of the dream analysis, involved the patient's primitive need to be both fed and impregnated by the father's genital products, revealing the patient's deeply impaired gender identity and, underlying that, her failed maternal identification.

In the case of idealization, the patient's message con-veys the following defensive communication: "You are wonderful, and because I esteem (love) you so much, you simply cannot find anything wrong with me, including my self-defeating and self-destructive behavior!"

Underlying this message is a more complex, transitivistic varia-tion of it based on projective identification (Grotstein 1981) and on the symbiotic component of the narcissistic transference. Thus, "Loving (admiring) you is the same as loving (admiring) myself; we are one together and you can't find fault with me because to do so would be to find fault with yourself." Contained in this message is the patient's need to unite or fuse with an *idealized parental image*, therewith to gain approbative mirroring for one's *grandiose-exhibitionistic self* as the so-called flip side of disapproval and devaluation expected from the idealized parental image derived from the projection of the patient's "bad objects" into the therapist.

In both cited cases (Mrs. G. – "acting in,") Miss J. – "acting out"), the detoxifying function of external controls for impulsive, potentially or actually self-injurious behavior, applied within outpatient processes, were sufficient to curb the behavior. When an outpatient process cannot, hospitalization is required to curb it before expressive psychotherapy can begin with many cases in the borderline-narcissistic spectrum of personality disorders (Meissner 1988, Rinsley 1980a).

Chapter 11

Beyond Idealization and Devaluation

The majority of personality-disordered cases amenable to psychoanalytic treatment belong within the borderline-narcissistic spectrum or continuum (Adler 1981, 1985, Grinker et al. 1968, Grinker and Werble 1977, Kernberg 1980, 1984, Kohut 1977, Meissner 1984, 1988, Rinsley 1982a, 1984, 1985, 1988b, Stone 1980). The ultimate goal of their treatment is to uncover and assist the patient to work through, hence to resolve the very early abandonment depression, with its attendant separation anxiety, that lies at the root of their character pathology (Masterson 1976, Masterson and Rinsley 1975, Rinsley 1982b). Thus, the treatment must address the patient's pathologically persistent symbiosis, with its various manifestations of failure of separation–individuation. Although the treatment must also appropriately address issues based on oedipal conflicts, it must nonetheless function in accordance with the fact that the patient's psychopathology reflects and results from primary developmental arrest, and not from regression from failure to resolve those conflicts.

Although it cannot be gainsaid that traumatogenic conflicts play an important role in the pathogenesis of cases of borderline and narcissistic personality disorders, it needs to be borne in mind that the conflicts are of a pre-oedipal nature. The conflicts, and the traumas associated with them, result from parental depersonification of the child (Rinsley 1971, 1980c, 1985) such that the parent, predominantly or exclusively the mother, perceives the child as someone or something other than who the child really is. Thus, as noted, depersonification lies at the basis of the mother's message to the borderline-to-be child that to separate is to perish, and of the mother's message to the narcissist-to-be child that he or she must become an adult before ever having been a child.

The complex psychostructural and adaptive encumbrances that the borderline or narcissistic patient carries with him into treatment are reflected in the profound ambivalence with which he approaches the therapeutic situation. This ambivalence is reflected in the apparent paradox of his urgent need for relief from the enormous burden of his psychopathology and his equally urgent need to defeat the therapist's efforts to create the conditions under which that relief may be obtained. The dialectical clash between his truncated need to grow and the pathological pull of his unresolved symbiosis colors almost everything he does or does not do throughout the early and middle phases of his treatment, until the point is reached at which a therapeutic alliance has begun to develop and, as a consequence, the resolution of his pathology has set in.

John B., an intellectually gifted 16-year-old, a few weeks away from discharge from full-time residential treatment, articulated it well during the 208th hour of his individual psychotherapy, which had begun shortly following the completion of his post-admission work-up:

P: "I did all those crazy things because I wanted to hurt myself."

T: "Anybody else?"

P: "Oh yeah, my mother, too."

T: "I think we both understand now why you needed to do that."

P: "Well, I wanted to get back at her—I wanted to make her feel real lousy."

T: "Your *real* mother?"

P: "No, not my real mother, the mother I had inside me, you know, the one in my head."

T: "How could you take it out on her and yourself too?"

P: "Well, that's because I really couldn't tell the difference—I didn't really know who I was, her or me!"

T: "You hadn't separated from her and she was inside you all the time."

P: "Yup, there she was, doin' her thing in there!"

T: "What about real mom?"

P: "Well, she's really not so bad. We understand each other a lot better now."

This youngster, diagnosed as suffering from narcissistic personality disorder and dysthymic disorder, had been in intensive residential treatment for a little over two years and in intensive analytic treatment for almost as long again as part of his overall care. His statements in the foregoing excerpt strikingly illustrate one of the essential ingredients of endopsychic structural change, i.e., the "assimilation" or "metabolization" of primitive introjects, in his case the mother's untransmuted, evocable image, as described by Jacobson (1964) and Kernberg (1966) and referred to by Fairbairn (1941) as the "dichotomy and exteriorization" of such introjects, thereby rendering them as "real." John could assimilate his "raw" maternal introject into his progressively mature, sublimatory "inner controls," while at the same time perceiving the mother figure "outside himself" in terms of the reality principle.*

As self psychology has demonstrated, the successful analytic treatment of these cases depends on the therapist's or analyst's sensitive, empathic attunement vis-à-vis the patient, which sets in motion a latter-day manifestation of the mutual cueing or communicative matching (Mahler 1968) between mother and child that essentially failed to occur when it should have. Like the latter, both the "real" and transferential features of the therapeutic relationship, as it proceeds to evolve into a genuine therapeutic alliance, promote the progressive assimilation of the patient's primitive introjects, most especially that of the prepotent figure of the mother, thereby catalyzing the development

---

*Fairbairn's "dichotomy and exteriorization" corresponds more than slightly to Kernberg's concept of the differentiation of self- and object representations that characterize his Stage 4 in the development of internalized object relations (see Chapter 15).

of object constancy with the resulting enhancement of the patient's ability to self-regulate his affectomotor discharges, hence to establish control over his symptomatic behavior.

Of course, parental attunement to the child's needs, dominated as they are by the pleasure principle, is never perfect. Were this not so, the child would never come to an awareness of the discomfort associated with their episodically unavoidable frustration; hence the child would not develop motivation to seek out ways to meet them himself. Optimal balance is the issue here.

The psychotherapeutic process serves as a prime arena where these issues, centering on the psychopathogenetic effects of failed parental empathy, depersonification, and seriously impaired object permanency and object constancy are played out (Adler 1985, Rinsley 1984, 1985, 1986). As Adler (1985) has pointed out, the borderline patient struggles endlessly to ward off the self-dissolutive fragmentation attendant upon his dysregulated affectomotor experiences, which undergo resurgence in the wake of the patient's inability to summon up an inner image of the therapist's or analyst's face (prosopagnosia), the hallmark of seriously impaired object permanency. When this occurs, as it frequently does in periods between therapeutic sessions, the patient will often attempt to ward off the impending regression by means of frantic or near-frantic efforts to contact the therapist day or night by telephone calls or even by appearing at the therapist's home or office. Again, the patient may, and often does, indulge in any of numerous varieties of obviously self-defeating and self-destructive behavior, such as getting into bouts of fisticuffs and drunkenness, drunk driving, other socially outrageous acts, and overt suicidal gestures, which represent misplaced efforts to provoke rescue by the therapist, thereby to revivify the therapist's image. When such efforts fail to remobilize the temporarily extinguished image of the therapist, or even when the patient does not indulge in them for whatever reasons, a terrifying descent into psychotic experience often follows (micropsychosis). Within the therapeutic situation, the patient will frequently "act in" by means of passive-aggressive, overtly disruptive, or other outrageous behavior in order to provoke regulatory controls from the therapist, but must reject them because submission to them implies a measure of personal growth, and growth threatens disaster.

In the case of the narcissistic personality, the major struggle concerns the preservation of a very fragile sense of self, of metastable inner coherence, for the less than adequate maintenance of which the powerful, adultomorphizing maternal introject is responsible. In such cases, the patient seeks approbative mirroring from the therapist or analyst, but must in various ways manage to reject it, especially early in the therapeutic process, lest such mirroring threaten to displace the maternal introject that has forbidden any meaningful object relationship other than with itself.

Especially during the early stages of treatment, these phenomena are repetitively recapitulated within the therapeutic transference. And again, as in the case of even the most sensitively empathic parent, the therapist's empathic attunement to the patient must necessarily fail from time to time. With the borderline patient, especially early in the treatment when external controls are needed to curb the patient's symptomatic acting out, the therapist conveys his empathic failure by failing to impose them despite the patient's overt verbal and nonverbal resistances to them. Empathic failure also ensues when such controls are excessive, hence suppressive of otherwise nonpathological, nonsymptomatic behavior, an antitherapeutic situation often found in inadequate inpatient or residential programs for children and adolescents, where behavior control becomes an end in itself.

Thus the therapeutic dilemma: controls seek to enforce internalization (identification), internalization signifies growth, and growth augurs for disaster; conversely, failure to impose needed controls leaves the patient at the mercy of his inner storms, which likewise augur for disaster. In the case of the higher-level narcissistic personality, empathic failure signifies a disruption of approbative mirroring, which the patient needs to an excessive degree in order to maintain his fragile sense of inner coherence. The frequency and fluidity of mutual projective identifications within the therapeutic transference–countertransference situation threaten to provoke affectomotor dysregulation in the therapist as well as resurgent narcissistic-mirroring needs that generate a therapeutic tightrope and are prone to leave the therapist with feelings of rage, depression, and physical exhaustion.

An example of the vicissitudes of projective identification in these cases found expression in the disruptive behavior of Mr. B., a middle-aged, successful businessman diagnosed as suffering from borderline personality disorder with narcissistic traits. The disruptive behavior occurred during an early-on therapeutic hour with a young, relatively inexperienced male therapist. As the hour drew to a close, the therapist announced that the hourly fee would be increased following the next hour, explaining that this was due to an increase in fee schedules imposed by the clinic's fiscal service. The patient promptly "blew up," hurling a spate of obscene invectives at the therapist, following which he noisily stomped out of the office, slamming the door behind him, leaving the therapist stunned and chagrined.

The next hour, the patient sheepishly reappeared and in a very subdued fashion apologized for his previous outburst. In exploring the possible basis for the patient's untoward behavior, the therapist said to the patient, "I wonder if my announcing the fee increase was what really provoked you," whereupon the patient retorted, "Hell no, the money didn't matter, but I thought *you* set the fee—who's in charge here, you or the goddam money people?"

In a later consultant's case conference that focused on the therapist's work with this patient, the following dialogue took place:

C: "What were your feelings when the patient lost control and left so abruptly?"

T: "It really shocked me. He took me by surprise. I felt really put down and that I'd missed the boat somewhere."

C: "What do you think really got him going?"

T: "I'm not sure. I thought it was the fee change. Money is very important to him. He told me once that he turns every coin over three times before he spends it. But I think that maybe that wasn't it."

C: "Well, leaving the 'turning-over-the-coin-in-the-hand' metaphor for the moment, what about his comment about who was really in charge?"

T: "Oh, now I see! He wanted me to be omnipotent! That

must be what he meant about who's in charge! Hmm—did I trash out his idealizing transference?"

C: "I think so. So why do you think he came back the next hour looking subdued and contrite?"

T: "Well, he must have felt guilty over what he did and he needed to make reparation for it, to make certain he really hadn't warded me off or even destroyed me so he wouldn't have provoked abandonment."

C: "Correct. He blew up when he quickly sensed that you were not in control of the process when you told him that some shadowy other person had been setting the fee. Your lack of control signified *his* loss of control of his preeruptive emotions. In effect, he felt you had abandoned him to some faceless, unknown other. As you've pointed out, his idealizing transference fell apart in one fell swoop!"

T: "I see that now."

C: "Let's go back to your earlier comment that it was the fee change itself that set him off."

T: "Well, he's an avaricious, cold-blooded business type and money is his God Almighty."

C: "Yes. For him, money, control, achievement, indeed his very self are all bound up together, the anal component of his personality. So when he came back and attempted to make reparation in Melanie Klein's sense, he was also indulging in what amounted to an exchange of goods, in Karl Abraham's sense."

T: "I see that."

C: "Now, one other thing. I suspect that you had some feelings when you were telling him about the fee increase."

T: "Hmm, let me think about that a minute. Hmm, yes, I think I'm onto something! I think I can recall feeling some sort of pleasure at the time, hmm!"

C: "A sort of triumph?"

T: "Yes, yes, that's what it was! I was hitting him where it hurts with the money thing."

C: "Do you find it hard to like this man?"

T: "Ah, I think I see what you're getting at! Well, I must admit that I find it difficult to like or empathize with people like him."

C: "Well, I think you told us that with the words 'avaricious,' 'cold-blooded,' and 'money is his God Almighty.'"

T: "So my attitude toward people like him managed to come across to him when I told him about the fee increase!"

C: "Yes, you sort of attacked him with that while you were indicating your impotence regarding not being in charge all at the same time."

In capably following up this exchange, the therapist's efforts led to an uncovering of a number of related themes that proved to be highly significant for an understanding of the patient's outburst as well as his pathology more generally. Not unexpectedly, it developed that, not only had the patient strongly idealized the therapist, but as well had felt responsible for what he perceived as the therapist's lack of control, epitomized in the incident regarding the fee change. The patient's outburst and abrupt departure from the hour could be seen to convey an aggressive attempt to disavow the therapist's purported ineffectuality, and the patient's guilt-laden responsibility for it, by running away. Finally, the patient's departure could be seen to represent an attempt to protect the therapist from further injury to his idealized image.

A most important accrual derived from further analysis of these matters was the patient's growing awareness, aided by appropriate transference interpretations, that he had been recapitulating vis-à-vis the therapist almost identical earlier experiences with his parents. The latter had been coldly aloof, his father having been in particular both emotionally unavailable and physically abusive to him. The patient had long since repressed the belief that his (the patient's) badness had rendered his father into a wimp who took it out on his son. The patient's mother, not surprisingly, had adultomorphized him as her "little man," clearly preferring him to the patient's father. Accordingly, much of the basis for the patient's inordinately aggressive cut-throat business practices could be seen to be derived from reaction–formation to his father's basic ineffectuality and from his need to gratify his adultomorphizing mother, all of which he had accomplished within a familial setting of emotional aloofness that characterized his emotional life since his childhood.

Chapter 12

The Patient's Protection of the Therapist

Often overlooked and of great significance for any comprehensive understanding of the therapeutic process with borderline and narcissistic personalities is the patient's need to safeguard or protect, indeed to "treat" the therapist or analyst (Malin and Grotstein 1966, Milner 1969, Searles 1967, 1979, Singer 1971, Whitaker and Malone 1953). In some instances of patient protective behavior toward the therapist, the aim is to attempt to undo harm that the patient believes has already been done to the therapist. These manifestations express the patient's urge to make reparation to the therapist, to repair the damage felt to have been visited on the "good object" therapist (actually, the therapist's good internal objects). Terrifyingly, within the context of the symbiotic (merger) component of the transference, damage to the therapist's good internal objects means damage to one's own good internal objects, signifying an attack on the patient's internalized good objects by his internalized bad objects (Fairbairn 1941, 1944). Insofar as damage to the therapist's good objects, hence to one's own good objects, threatens to leave a preponderance of bad objects, the patient is accordingly left with a congeries of self-generated persecutors that must be neutralized or effaced at all cost. To this situation the patient may respond in a variety of ways.

He may redouble his efforts to idealize the therapist, to convert the therapist into an all-good figure in order to disavow the preponderance of bad objects. Thus, the patient may assume an attitude of defensive pseudocompliance in an effort to bring about closeness to the overidealized therapist. Such an effort, however, may bring about the opposite effect.

The therapist may unwittingly respond with undue (counter-transferential) embarrassment, indicative of his view of himself as unworthy of the patient's amative profferings. The patient then comes to view the therapist's need to distance himself emotionally as a move toward disengagement, rejection, and abandonment, leading to various manifestations of acting in or acting out.

A striking example of this occurred during the third year of a "classical" analysis of a mid-thirties, unmarried professional woman who had been struggling for some time with strong sexual feelings for her male analyst. The analyst was evidently unaware of the strength of the patient's feelings for him and in responding to them inappropriately, the following interaction took place (paraphrased from secondarily reported material from the particular analytic hour in which it had occurred):

P: "Well, I think I'm ready for an intimate relationship with a man again. What do you think?"

A: "Yes, I agree. You've made good progress in coming to terms with your problems with your father and other men."

P: "You really mean that?"

A: "Yes, of course."

P: "Well, f____k you! To hell with you! I'm done! I'm never coming back here!" (Other unrecorded invectives followed, and the patient departed the office and terminated the analysis.)

Several years later, when the patient had been in analytic psychotherapy with me for some fifty-five hours, she could begin to work through what had happened so dramatically in that terminal hour of her prior analysis. (The following reported dialogue is approximate but close to what was actually said, as I did not keep detailed notes for this part of the hour. The reader will not long be in the dark concerning my failure to make and keep such notes!)

T: "All right, so now you understand much more about why you bolted out of your analysis."

P: "Yes, I think so. My feelings for him were very strong, and I felt he was putting me off, getting rid of me by agreeing that I could be sexually involved with somebody else."

T: "You mean somebody other than he."

P: "Yes."

T: "So you abandoned him in order to control his abandonment of you as you saw it."

P: "Yes, that's exactly what I did. I see that it was the wrong thing to do."

T: "What else could there be about your feeling that your analyst couldn't handle your sexual feelings for him?"

P: "I'll tell you. It meant he couldn't handle me *at all*! He couldn't really help me with any of my problems, not just the sexual part of me!"

In this case, further analysis revealed that the patient's abrupt termination of her prior treatment process served yet another purpose in addition to her need to ward off and control a fantasied abandonment by her analyst. It also served to spare the analyst further contact with her bad objects, which had long been associated with her sexuality, in effect to protect him from them. She could later say, "I think I was afraid that he would respond sexually to me even though I wanted him to and he'd be like all the other men I went to bed with!" As the reader will duly note, this patient's view of men, hence of her male analyst, was in many ways similar to that of Mrs. G. cited above.

Thus, as illustrated by the foregoing case, the patient may abscond from the therapy in order to safeguard or protect the therapist.

Again, the patient may engage in various kinds of grossly inappropriate or even outrageous forms of social behavior outside the therapeutic process (acting out) or within the therapeutic process (acting in) in an effort to provoke actual abandonment by the therapist, hence termination of the therapy. The message here is, "I'm so bad, so awful a person, that it is a waste of your time to attempt to treat me." Various forms of self-endangering behavior may express this message, the most extreme example of which is the suicidal gesture or, most ominously, a serious suicidal attempt. Paradoxically, in such cases, the patient's associated, underlying rescue fantasy is not difficult to discern.

The patient's need to protect, treat, or even heal the therapist recapitulates the young child's infantile–grandiose self-perception that he is responsible for any and all untoward happenings to his parents, including separations, divorces, illnesses, and parental deaths. Accordingly, he must make reparation in order to undo these occurrences, to reconstitute or regenerate the damaged or lost parental figures and the flow of supplies from them. The resistance aspect of the patient's protectiveness and guilty self-blame may imply the following:

It perpetuates the patient's view of himself as a bad, evil, destructive person whose badness is beyond the therapist's helpful ministrations; hence, the therapy is foredoomed to failure.

It serves to maintain in repression the pathologically persistent symbiosis, hence the separation–individuation arrest that underlies patient's psychopathology, thereby rendering them inaccessible to the therapeutic process.

It serves to perpetuate the patient's pleasurably sadistic view of himself, related to his underlying grandiosity, as a fiendishly potent being capable of utterly devastating any effort by the therapist to invade and vitiate his pathological internalized object relations.

Finally, the need to protect the therapist invariably in part derives from a core of healthy magnanimity deeply concealed behind the welter of antitherapeutic transference manifestations. This positive aspect of the patient's hidden real self (Winnicott 1960) needs to be recognized by the therapist, along with confrontative, clarifying, and interpretive efforts directed toward its resistance-related aspects.

As in the case of Mrs. G. (*supra*), the therapist needs to give evidence that he recognizes the good or benevolent core of the patient's protectiveness. A further example is illustrated by the following dialogue involving Mr. Y., a 34-year-old disc jockey with narcissistic personality disorder:

T: "I have the impression that your missing some hours and coming late to others is somehow your way of not wanting to do something bad to me."

P: "Well, I'm a pretty bad fellow, you know!"

T: "Let's discuss that some more."

P: "Well, I think that when you really got to know me, you wouldn't want anything to do with me. That reminds me of Groucho Marx, who said he wouldn't want to join any club that would have him as a member."

T: "But what about your not wanting to do something bad or harmful to me? We've discussed that in the past, and we need to look at it more."

P: "Well, you'd naturally want to get away from that, wouldn't you? Just like everybody else in my life!"

T: "We certainly need to explore further how you came to have such a poor opinion of yourself, but I have to tell you something I believe is true about you."

P: "Er, what?"

T: "I think that you've been missing and delaying our hours because you have a deep concern for me, but this doesn't fit together with your acknowledged need for treatment, so you're caught in a bind."

P: "Hmm. Imagine—me a nice guy! Yeah, I've got to admit it, I think you're right, but boy, is it hard for me to say that! I'm not used to thinking of myself that way."

T: "What about that?"

P: "Well, I was always a bad-ass kid when I was growing up—lots of trouble, lots of fights. My father used to say 'You're a little bastard—you're gonna die in prison!' "

T: "What about the pet alligator you had?"

P: "Oh, him! The little bastard used to snap at me and hiss at me, but I took good care of him."

T: "What eventually happened to him?"

P: "Well, when he got too big for me to handle, I took him to a pet store and they kept him and I never found out what happened to him. I think they sent him to a zoo or something."

T: "What did your parents think about the alligator?"

P: "Well, they never told me to get rid of him. My father used to say, 'That's a bad-ass animal just like you!' "

T: "Could I be a bad-ass animal just like you?"

P: "Wait a minute! Hold on! *You* like *me* and Stanley (*the alligator*)?"

T: "Well?"

P: "Oh, now I get it! So you're like Stanley and I need to take care of you!"

T: "As long as I don't bite you, eh?"

P: "Yeah!"

T: "I'll bet you missed Stanley when you finally had to part with him."

P: "Yeah, I sure did, but I never let anybody know about how I felt. I never cried."

T: "So, do we know something about your missing hours and all that?"

P: "Well, I don't cry when I stay out of here. Usually I feel good about not having to come in here and do this sort of thing. But then, I sort of regret not coming, and, you know, I always come back."

Over the ensuing several hours, the patient arrived on time, and with a few more delinquencies over the following

several months, became prompt in his attendance. In the foregoing excerpt, it can be seen that the therapist's pursuit of the
issue of the patient's protectiveness toward him uncovered exceptionally important material related to his difficulty in
mourning separations and losses, as exemplified in the patient's
nurturant relationship with, and eventual separation from, his
pet alligator.

Chapter 13

Empathic Failure, Abandonment, and Mourning

The core pathogenetic role of abandonment, most evident in the borderline personality but also operative in the narcissistic personality, was emphasized early (Masterson and Rinsley 1975). This work underscored the resistance against abandonment depression served by these patients' symptomatic behavior.

The subjective state conveyed by the term [abandonment depression] includes a core anxiety component and a more differentiated component. The former is of an instinctual quality and corresponds with the primal experience of impending loss of the maternal stimulus barrier against endopsychic and external stimulation, with ensuing gross ego trauma. The latter, more structuralized, conveys the feeling of guilt which signifies the ego's anxiety over impending "abandonment" or sadistic assault by the superego, also perceived as a threatened loss or withdrawal of supplies. The basic feelings common to the state of abandonment depression comprise *a profound sense of emptiness* and, as an aspect of estrangement, a sense of meaninglessness of the "external world." [Masterson and Rinsley 1975, p. 170]

As previously noted, another and better term for abandonment depression would therefore be *dysphoric separation anxiety*, the psychological sword of Damocles that hangs over the existence of the personality-disordered patient. Also as noted, its pathological persistence forms the basis for the patient's failure to have worked through the depressive position, with a resultant incapacity to mourn.

The capacity to mourn or grieve requires the use of evocative memory, that is, the ability to call to mind and to work over and through the internal images of "lost" objects (Freud 1914b, 1917). As noted before, evocative memory is profoundly deficient in borderline personalities and is insufficiently drive-reducing (tension-easing) in narcissistic personalities.

It may now be noted that the therapist's episodic, unavoidable empathic failures, which signify for the patient an interruption of grandiose-exhibitionistic mirroring and of the therapist's unavailability as an idealized parental image, evoke abandonment depression for a number of reasons:

In borderline cases, empathic failure threatens the patient with total extinguishment of the therapist's extremely tenuous image and function as a holding-soothing introject (Adler 1985), leading to internal and external ego boundary disruption (Federn 1952) and the patient's feeling that he is falling apart (micropsychosis). To ward this off, the patient may, and often does, indulge in an exacerbation of his usual self-defeating, self-destructive symptomatic behavior.

In cases of narcissistic personality disorder, resurgent abandonment depression resulting from empathic failure is perceived as a major insult to the patient's tenuously maintained sense of self-esteem. Here the perceived sudden loss of the therapist's mirroring and idealized parental function removes the therapist's service as a bulwark against the patient's powerful maternal superego introject, which now proceeds to assault the ego by direct, sadistic attacks and by threats to withdraw needed supplies.* The clinical symptoms that result include resurgent depression alternating with behavior based on the reevoked manic defenses — boredom and ennui, various degrees of melancholia and nihilism, admixed with intense envy and greed and manic-like hyperactivity.

Everyday life is replete with numerous comings and goings, arrivals and departures and, at times, traumas

---

*The important relationship between depression and impairment or loss of self-esteem was cogently pointed out by Bibring (1953) and recently restated by Morrison (1983), who has drawn attention to the similarity of Bibring's view and Kohut's concept of depletion of the self in narcissistic cases.

associated with major interpersonal losses. Such comings
and goings are difficult enough for psychotic and borderline individuals, and major losses pose well-nigh insuperable difficulties for them as a consequence of seriously
impaired evocative memory (object impermanency).
Again, as noted, inasmuch as unimpaired evocative
memory is essential for the productive use of fantasy, and
since fantasy forms the basis for effective foreplanning,
fantasy deficiency (alexithymia) disarticulates the individual's perceptual awareness of the smooth flow of time from
past to present moment to future. The result is a chaotic
sense of ambiguity and unpredictability in relation to external figures and events.

Well known in this regard are patients' episodes of
psychological disorganization in the wake of the therapist's
vacations, late arrivals at the therapeutic sessions, failures
to acknowledge the patient as a passerby on the street, and
the like. Again, in the same category are patient's demanding, imploring telephone calls at all hours in an effort to
reconstitute the fading or extinguished inner image of the
therapist, therewith to ward off impending regressive experiences.

Considered in wider environmental terms, empathic
failure may be understood in terms of the individual's
failure to have achieved and maintained a congruous relationship with the "outside" generally. The concept self-
outside congruity is inherent in Hartmann's (1939) notion
of the "average expectable environment" and in Winnicott's
(1965) concept of the good enough mother as the major
articulator of what he has termed the *facilitating environment*. Related concepts are Kohut's (1977) mirroring, Mah-

ler's (1968) mutual cueing and mirroring frame of reference and Bion's (1967) notion of the container-contained maternal function. All of these recognize the indispensability of the environment's nurturant or alimentational function as necessary for the individual's overall psychosocial growth, as well as his psychological integrity at any given moment.

Considered in this more extended sense, empathic failure may be rapidly communicated by means of sudden, unheralded, or unanticipated changes in environmental conditions, such as alterations in illumination, temperature, arrangement of furniture, and the like. Among those individuals who respond traumatically to such changes are schizophrenics, those with moderate to severe organic dementia, autistic children, and borderline preadults and adults. Their urgent need for environmental immutability is a consequence of pathological concretism, that is, the inability to flexibly shift attentive focus, a major component of what Goldstein (1939, 1959) termed *concrete attitude*. Their autonomically based emotional outbursts (Goldstein's *catastrophic reactions*) resulting from environmental change are latter-day manifestations of the spontaneous affectomotor storm–rage reactions of unattended infants (Mahler 1965), which require the equivalent of nurturant maternal ministrations to be damped down and put to rest.

A graphic example of such catastrophic decompensations occurred one dark, gloomy day in the day room of an adolescent inpatient ward for psychotic and borderline youngsters. All at once, electric power was temporarily lost and the ward was plunged into darkness. Immediately, several patients became acutely disorganized and disoriented, began to cry, shout, and run about, and required immediate staff intervention to calm themselves.

Freud's classic 1916 paper, devoted to the negative therapeutic reaction, persons "wrecked by success" and criminals from a sense of guilt, conveyed his early and highly sensitive insight into these varieties of self-defeating, self-destructive behavior as guilt-suffused responses to an internalized nonfacilitating environment. The case of the recidivistic criminal is especially apposite. By means of repetitive antisocial acts that provoke apprehension, arraignment, trial, and incarceration, he succeeds in getting himself confined within a uterine edifice constructed of concrete walls and iron bars, within which he obtains the external controls he otherwise protests and abhors. Here are extreme examples of a form of perverse communicative matching lacking in the elements of Winnicott's facilitating environment, except in those cases for whom incarceration leads to the offender's psychosocial rehabilitation.

Chapter 14

Mirroring, Empathy, and the Rapprochement Subphase

The concept of a mirroring stage of infant development was put forward by the French psychoanalyst Jacques Lacan (1949). He noted that the recognition of oneself in the mirror image begins at about 6 months of age and profoundly affects ego development throughout the ensuing year; thus, the mirroring stage continues from the sixth through the eighteenth month. It is significant that Lacan's mirroring stage coincides with Mahler's differentiation, practicing, and beginning rapprochement subphases of separation–individuation (Mahler et al. 1975). It is during this period that the growing child's object relations evolve from a condition of (symbiotic) undifferentiation of self- and object-images toward their beginning differentiation, as epitomized in the rapprochement crisis. Significant also is the fact that object permanency, that is, the capacity for evocative memory, is ordinarily in place by 18 months, with the attainment of object constancy by 36 months. Lacan emphasizes the developmental importance of the child's ability to differentiate his nascent self-image from his mirror image, thereby strengthening his transition from a condition of perceptual transitivism toward the inception of an awareness of his own reality, hence of his sense of reality.

During these early months, the mother's nurturant mirroring plays a pivotal role in promoting the child's evolving self-differentiation. By serving as an external re- flector, she promotes the child's self-objectification as he comes to perceive that his mirror image and her object- image are not the same, nor are they the same as his subjective self-image. These fundamental differentiations begin in earnest during the practicing subphase (10–16 months), coincident with the child's approach–avoidance, arrival–departure behavior vis-à-vis the mother, and with his associated need for repetitive libidinal refueling, as expressed in his looking and crawling back to her to recapture her as yet evanescent image. During the rap- prochement subphase (16–26 months), the child's evolving capacity for evocative memory will proceed to consolidate that image toward its emergence as a reliably verifiable percept. Along with that will proceed a consolidation of his self-image as it progressively differentiates from the evoked maternal image. Of great importance during the rapprochement subphase is the child's need to involve the mother in cooperative activities in which he proceeds to imitate and internalize the mother's skills during their cooperative activities together.

These pristine developmental phenomena and interactions come to be reflected and reenacted in the course of analytic treatment. Self psychology's emphasis on empathic attunement reflects the very early goodness of fit or communicative matching between mother and child, and the therapeutic alliance has its origin in the residues of the shared parent–child activities of the rapprochement subphase. The personality-disordered patient's transferential idealizing and devaluing maneuvers and his grandiose-exhibitionistic blandishments during the early and middle phases of treatment are easily noted to represent a recapitulation of essentially the same needs and actions so evident during the child's infantile years. It should be noted, in addition, that the patient's negativistic and devaluing maneuvers and communications during therapeutic sessions also convey the infant's otherwise healthy need to say No, thereby to express his growing differentiation from the mother by exerting an increasingly independent impact on her and on his environment generally (Spitz 1957). In view of these facts, the logic of Kohut's position on empathy appears irrefutable.

During much of the early and middle stages of the treatment of these patients, the therapist or analyst finds himself involved, if not indeed immersed, in preverbal transferential and countertransferential experiences that reflect both traumatic and nontraumatic occurrences that have characterized the patient's life as a very young child. Ultimately, the successful therapeutic process recapitulatively moves through latter-day manifestations of the differentiation and practicing subphases, in terms of which the patient's idealizing, devaluing, and grandiose-exhibitionistic maneuvers can be understood. The elements of a genuine therapeutic alliance begin to coalesce when the therapy has proceeded into a recapitulated rapprochement subphase, and the patient has begun in earnest to work it through. It is only then that the therapist and the patient really start to work together.

Chapter 15

Cure

The word *cure*, from the Latin *cura* (care or healing) finds little use among psychiatrists, psychoanalysts, and other allied mental health workers. In general medicine, it applies only to certain infectious, parasitic, and surgical disorders, with the remainder subject only to various degrees of palliation or symptomatic remission. In the psychiatric realm, many hold that cure, meaning the total removal of the psychopathological process and its attendant symptomatology, can never be accomplished. It is widely known, however, that major psychotic symptomatology often remits spontaneously, and that many antisocial personalities no longer display their untoward behavior upon entering the period of middle life. Eysenck (1967) has stated that a majority of cases of psychoneurosis eventually remit without treatment and may indeed actually fare better if kept out of the psychotherapist's hands.

It is possible to apply the term *cure* in the case of the major personality disorders? I believe it is, if one qualifies the term in accordance with what is known of their dynamic pathogenesis. Adler (1985) points out that the successful treatment of borderline personalities causes them to acquire the characteristics of narcissistic personalities. The successful treatment of the narcissistic personality results in the emergence of psychoneurosis or even of a personality that can be considered healthy. How can this point of view be justified?

We may begin by considering Kernberg's (1972) concept of the progressive development of internalized object relations. In psychosis, which corresponds with Kernberg's Stages 1 and 2, the infant's self- and object–representations are essentially undifferentiated, and his world is organized in terms of the pleasure principle. This state of endopsychic affairs may be diagrammed as follows:

$$\begin{array}{c|c} G & B \\ \hline S\text{--}O & S\text{--}O \end{array}$$

where G = all good, B = all bad, S = self–representation, and O = object–representation; the symbolism S-O may

be rendered as *self–object(s)*.* Stages 1 and 2 roughly corre-
spond chronologically with Mahler's autistic and symbiotic
phases and the early part of the differentiation subphase of
separation–individuation (birth through the first postnatal
year), which also corresponds with the classical oral stage of
psychosexual development.

As the child proceeds through the subsequent differentiation and practicing subphases (6–16 months), self–
and object–representations begin to differentiate, again in
accordance with the all good-all bad pleasure principle.
This process reaches its peak during the rapprochement
subphase (16–26 months), which corresponds with Kernberg's Stage 3. It may be diagrammed as follows:

$$
\begin{array}{c|c}
G & B \\
\hline
S & S \\
O & O
\end{array}
$$

Finally, self– and object–representations become differentiated for the most part, the previously split-off good-
bad self– and object–representations begin to assume the
features of whole-object representations (M. Klein 1935,
1946), and the reality principle now begins to replace the

---

*The question arises concerning how to square Kernberg's view of the development of
internalized object relations, specifically his concept of the differentiation of self– and
object–representations, with Kohut's view of selfobjects as persistent throughout life. The
answer is provided by Fairbairn (1954), whose concept of dynamic structures anticipated
Kohut's selfobjects and who explicated self–object differentiation in terms of the exter-
nalization of the object, therby establishing it as real. There is no genuine conflict
between Kernberg's and Kohut's views when it is recognized that, in Fairbairn's terms, all
mental representations possess self-representational features.

pleasure principle. These transformations may be dia-grammed as follows:

$$\begin{array}{c|c} S & O \\ \hline G & G \\ B & B \end{array}$$

This is Kernberg's Stage 4 of object-relations development, with its replacement of splitting by normal repression; beginning working-through of the depressive position with inception of the capacity to mourn; development of object permanency, thus laying the foundation for the later development of libidinal object constancy; and entrance into the oedipal stage.

These achievements, which characterize the healthily developing child's preschool years, also characterize the progress of the successfully treated borderline personality. The result is the emergence of the narcissistic personality, during the course of whose subsequent treatment a further consolidation of these transformations will occur, leading to a transition to a condition of essentially healthy whole-object relations.*

Within the context of these formulations, therefore, cure may be said to apply to psychotic patients whose treatment has brought them from Kernberg's Stages 1 and 2 to his Stage 3 and to borderline and some lower-level narcissistic personalities whose treatment has brought

*For a further, detailed discussion of how whole-objects develop from part-objects, considered in terms of Fairbairn's object-relations formulations, see Rinsley (1982a, 1987, 1988c).

them from Stage 3 to Stage 4, as it were. In the case of the majority of higher-level narcissistic personalities, successful treatment carries them from a state of developmental arrest somewhere between Kernberg's Stages 3 and 4 into the developmental achievements of Stage 4 proper. These object-relations transformations (self psychologists would term them transmutations) constitute sweeping psycho-structural remodelings that have a lasting impact on the organization of the personality.

Chapter 16

The Achievement of Healthy Object Relations

As Adler (1985) has pointed out, the therapeutic establishment of the soothing-holding introject constitutes a necessary early step toward the borderline patient's achievement of stable internalized object relations. The borderline patient's transitivistic condition carries with it the terrifying implication that the extinguishment of the therapist's internalized image signifies the disappearance of the real therapist, whom the patient has abolished, leaving

the patient abandoned and riven by the most archaic form
of guilt for having done so. By the same token, once the
therapist's introject has become stable, hence evocable, the
therapist has concomitantly assumed the status of a real
personage in the outside world. This is the significance of
Fairbairn's dichotomy and exteriorization process: the dichotomy healthily involves the establishment of the
soothing-holding internalized image of the therapist, while
the exteriorization establishes and maintains the therapist
in reality.

The anlage of all evocable inner images, whether in a
state of psychological health or not, is the primal maternal
introject.* In the case of the borderline personality, that
introject assumes the form of a congeries of split-off, mutu-
ally antagonistic dynamic structures (Fairbairn 1954) that
have been termed the *split object-relations unit of the borderline* (Masterson and Rinsley 1975). The endopsychic cleav-
ages inherent in this sundered structure are responsible for
its evocative unreliability, hence its failure as a drive-
reducer.

In the case of the narcissistic personality, the primal
maternal introject is apparently less sundered, that is (in
Kohut's terms), it is stable if archaic, hence readily evocable

---

*Considerable controversy surrounds the nature of this (primal) introject. Kleinian
theory considers it to be a part-object, viz., the mother's breast, which becomes
transformed into a whole-object, viz., the mother herself, as a consequence of the
working-through of the depressive position (Klein 1935, 1940, 1946, 1948) and Mahlerian
phase theory is within this conceptual framework (Mahler 1968, Mahler et al. 1975). On
the other hand, Fairbairn (1954) considers the primal introject to be a whole-object-like
entity (his so-called "original object"), a view that is akin to that put forward by the
currently popular Daniel Stern (1985).

(object permanency). Nevertheless, its soothing-holding function is contingent on the patient's renunciation of all real object relationships, and when the prospect of such relationships materializes, the introject reverts to its attacking mode, assaulting and threatening withdrawal of supplies from the patient's ego.

> A young woman told her therapist, "Mother passed out our self-esteem each day. . . . We felt that if we left we would lose it . . . we always had to return for it and wait for it."
> McArthur cites the depersonifying "message" regularly transmitted to the future narcissistic personality: "(Y)ou must not dare to love anyone but me . . . . You will not have any emotional or physical need for anyone but me." [McArthur 1988, p. 12–15]

It may be seen, therefore, that the narcissistic personality's resistance to his treatment derives from his primal introject's interdiction of other object relationships, including, most poignantly, the therapist–patient relationship, the most "dangerous" of all encounters the patient may have. In successful cases, by means of the analysis of resistances and transference manifestations, energized by the judicious use of approbative mirroring by the therapist, the latter's image is gradually, even painstakingly internalized by the patient, and over time comes to displace the maternal introject as the patient's major mirroring and idealizing source of supplies. As a felicitous result, the patient's ability to utilize the therapist in this way proceeds to generalize to others, an early and necessary step toward the eventual generation of other meaningful object relationships.

One young woman in her early twenties put it nicely. Said she, "I never thought anybody would like me or approve of what I did other than my mother. I was always afraid of getting into relationships. Now I know you (therapist) like me and you don't disapprove of my friends."

A bright 16-year-old adolescent boy said, "My mother used to tell me not to trust anybody but her, and I got to believe that if anybody told me something good about myself they were up to something. I always thought that there's got to be something wrong with me if nobody else but her could like me."

The latter part of this boy's statement conveyed his long-standing feeling that there was something vaguely, ineffably wrong with him, hence that nobody but his mother could like him or honestly approve of anything he did. A high achiever academically, he had long immersed himself in very successful intellectual pursuits ("to please Mom"), which had garnered for him considerable praise, in which, paradoxically, he could never believe. Here was an evident clinical example of a particular self-percept that Balint (1968) termed *basic fault*.

Chapter 17

Basic Fault

Freud's (1916) self-defeating cases indulged in their various forms of self-ruinous behavior as a consequence of enormous guilt. Their antics in part represented efforts toward redemptive, reparative self-propitiation, to make up to an introjected parental–representational figure whom they believed they had injured or damaged, and for whose consequent retributive aggression against them they felt ultimately responsible. It was Michael Balint (1968) who drew attention to the fact that early failure of parent–child mutual attunement lay at the basis of the individual's chronic, vague sense that there was something that was somehow very wrong or defective about oneself. One result, which typified Freud's "exceptions" cases, involved the individual's chronic, repetitive indulgence of self-destructive or self-defeating behavior, including the negative therapeutic reaction, in a counter-phobic effort to gain mastery over feeling defective or bad by paradoxically proving that he really was no good.

A professional woman in her late thirties with the diagnoses of dysthymic disorder and narcissistic traits said, "I've always felt that there was something not right about myself, that there was something the matter with me. I could never figure out what it was, just that there was something missing or wrong."

The ensuing dialogue proved illuminating:

T: "Can you expand on that some more?"

P: "Oh, I think I know what you're getting at! My previous analyst thought it was because I didn't have a penis, that I wasn't born a boy."

T: "Is that all he said about that?"

P: "Well, he didn't say much about anything, but he seemed to think that that was what made me feel bad about myself."

T: "Don't you agree with that?"

P: "Well, I can admit that that's probably a part of why I felt bad about myself, but I think there's a lot more to it than my genitals."

T: "What about the 'a lot more'?"

P: "Well, it's like what's not right about me is that there's something inside me that's making me feel the way I do and I don't know what it is."

T: "Something, or *somebody?*"

P: "Hmm . . . somebody . . . hmm. Well, it's not me, that's for sure!"

T: "You can recognize that whatever 'it' is is not you, but it's like something or somebody foreign or alien inside you."

P: "Yes, that's the way it feels, but what could it be?"

The subsequent several hours were devoted to an ongoing analysis of the internalized "something" or "somebody." The sequence proceeded essentially as follows:

The foreign body turned out to be the patient's stern, rejecting father, with whom she had counterphobically identified much as would an oedipal boy. The "it" was revealed as the father's penis, which the little girl had cannibalistically introjected as a defense against her fear of it. Then came the introjective *pièce de résistance*, as it were: a condensed mother-with-a-breast (in reality, mother-with-a-penis) figure, which Fairbairn (1941) originally described as the maternal object during the late oral stage of infantile dependence. The patient could now begin to perceive the internalized foreign body, in her particular case, as a whole-object treated as a part-object, a fusion of male-paternal (penis) and female-maternal (breast) representations. Much later, ongoing work revealed that this primitive androgynous introject was derived from the vastly ungratifying mother–daughter relationship that had resulted from the mother's severe postpartum depression, which had persisted throughout the patient's preschool years, remanifested in the patient's own chronic depression and feelings of personal futility.

In this woman's case, *maternal introject* actually described an androgynous image with its condensed breast and phallic part-objects.

Chapter 18

Treatment Phases

Devotees of the game of chess traditionally divide it into three phases or stages, which they term *opening game*, *middle game*, and *end game*, and Freud (1913b) analogized the beginning of psychoanalytic treatment to the first of these. The concept of the triphasic nature of the course of treatment based on psychoanalytic principles was put forward by Masterson (1971, 1974, 1976) in the case of borderline adolescents and adults and by myself in the case of inpatient preadolescents and adolescents (Rinsley 1980a, d; see also Lewis 1970). Adler (1985) has postulated three phases in the analytic treatment of borderline personalities, and Kernberg and his colleagues detailed two phases in the treatment of borderline patients (Kernberg et al. 1989).

My own work with inpatient adolescents, like that of Masterson, described the course of intensive treatment in terms of an initial *resistance phase* (Masterson called it the *testing phase*) followed by a *middle, definitive,* or *introjective phase* (Masterson's *working-through phase*) and a final *resolution phase* (Masterson's *separation phase*). It appeared that the first two of these phases were respectively recapitulating a complex of psychological events that Bowlby (1953, 1960a,b, 1962) had described in the case of prematurely separated infants, namely, his stages of *protest* and *despair*; and in unsuccessfully treated cases, the third of our phases appeared to assume the features of Bowlby's stage of *detachment*.

In the case of hospitalized preadolescents and adolescents, the three phases bore the following characteristics:

Resistance (Testing) Phase. The hallmark of this phase of fulltime inpatient or residential treatment was resistance to the impact of the treatment staff and to the milieu generally. In the case of youngsters with borderline and narcissistic personality disorders, that is those suffering from various degrees of separation–individuation failure, this phase lasted for no less than one year following admission. The specific resistances assumed a wide variety of manifestations, ranging from adroit dissimulation through negativistic passive-aggressiveness to outright rebelliousness and destructiveness toward others and property (Rinsley and

Inge 1961). Their objective was to deflect therapeutic staff's attention away from the underlying abandonment depression and the pathologically persistent symbiosis associated with it. Concomitant with these resistance maneuvers went the parents', and particularly the mother's, transparently collusive efforts to abet them as the various manifestations of these efforts came to be expressed in the family treatment process (Rinsley and Hall 1962). The patients' and the parents' resistances were noted to express the specific and nonspecific structural characteristics of the borderline, particularly defenses centering on splitting (Kernberg 1977). The threats conveyed in the maternal messages to these youngsters were the same as those that could be identified in adult cases: in the case of the borderline youngster, abandonment to the strange treatment figures viewed as persecutors who would tear the youngster away from the symbiosis and thereby destroy one or both partners to it; in the case of the youngster with narcissistic personality disorder, assaultive abandonment by the powerful superego introject should the youngster begin to form any significant relationships with the treatment staff.

Middle (Definitive, Introjective, Working-Through) Phase. The patient's entrance into the ensuing middle phase of treatment was marked by the beginning waning of the resistance and early moves by the patient toward internalization of certain of the program's treatment figures and the milieu's operating rules. The term *introjective* reflects this beginning internalization. The term *working-through* signifies the emergence of the heretofore stringently guarded-against abandonment depression, which proceeds to assume a wide range of symptomatic expressions, ranging from manic-like acting out and major depression through assorted neurotic hysteriform, hypochondriacal, and somatizing manifestations. Indeed, the patient appeared to be "falling apart." At the same time, the ongoing internalizations of the staff good objects accompanied by the patient's projection into them of his bad objects has now begun in earnest. As a consequence, good and bad self- and object-representations have begun to differentiate and the working-through of the depressive position has gotten underway. Another 12 to 24 months of ongoing intensive treatment are generally required before the patient has substantially completed the tasks of this phase.

Resolution (Separation) Phase. Discharge from inpatient or residential treatment is the pragmatic goal of this phase of treatment. During it, the patient has completed the bulk of the work of the depressive position, has achieved a significant degree of the ability to sense and test reality, and has formed the basis for whole-object relations. A further period of postdischarge psychotherapy, including family therapy in some cases, is almost always needed to assist the patient and the family to consolidate the gains made during the extended period of the patient's inpatient treatment.

It is throughout the resistance phase of treatment that the imposition of strict but flexible external controls against acting out achieves its greatest importance. If the acting out assumes the form of loss of control of aggressive and erotic impulses, these need to be contained by both verbal and physical means as required, accompanied by suitable confrontation and clarification. If the acting out is expressed in withdrawal, passive-aggressiveness, and negativism, then various degrees of "push" are required to activate the patient toward staff and peer interactions. The staff need always to remember that acting out, no matter the form it assumes, conveys powerful transference meaning, and during this phase of treatment, clarification becomes the method *par excellence* for assisting the patient to develop whatever degree of understanding he may be capable of at the time. Thus, the major goal of resistance phase treatment is to convert symptomatic behavior into secondary process verbal communication between patient and staff, in Masterson's (1981) terms, to transform "transference acting out" into "transference." Within the inpatient or residential setting, the available educational, occupational-therapeutic, and recreational-therapeutic modalities become interpretive arms of the overall therapeutic process in conjunction with the "life space" format that pervades the overall milieu (Redl 1959a,b).

For the borderline patient, these endeavors catalyze the process by which the milieu as a whole and its various therapeutic figures evolve as an aggregate soothing-holding introject by means of which the patient begins to exert increasing degrees of inner control over his affectomotor dysregulation. Introduced at an appropriate time, usually later in the resistance phase when the patient has begun to adapt to the milieu, psychotherapy can serve as an important component of the overall therapeutic process.

For the patient with narcissistic personality disorder, these endeavors promote internalizations that signify to the patient that it is both possible and safe to develop and maintain meaningful relationships with objects other than the introjected adultomorphizing maternal figure.

During the middle or working-through (introjective) phase, these accomplishments go forward in increasing measure and depth. As the new introjects take increasingly firm hold as good objects, the elements of the split object-relations unit (bad self-objects) become progressively externalized, and with them the raw (unneutralized) affects comprising the dysphoric separation anxiety (abandonment depression) associated with them. As this occurs, the confrontative and clarifying therapeutic components of the overall milieu become increasingly interpretive in the genetic-dynamic sense, linking current transference manifestations with early, pathogenetic traumas and conflicts that form the basis for the patient's psychopathology. To that end, the formal psychotherapeutic process serves an indispensable function as it becomes progressively integrated with the overall expressive work that the milieu continues to address to the patient. As noted, this is almost always a difficult time for patient and staff alike. Transference and countertransference issues resurge as the patient externalizes his bad objects and projects them into the staff, thereby creating a congeries of fearful, powerful persecutors. But along with these also go the patient's combined feelings of helplessness and defensive omnipotence, and as these are winnowed, modified, and remodified, as they pass back and forth, the patient's self- and object-representations progressively differentiate and become more real. Now the persecutors, created as a consequence of the patient's projections, turn out to be—*mirabile dictu*—benevolent, hence trustworthy. As the patient's all good-all bad splitting passes from the psychological scene as his self- and object-representations progressively differentiate, the heretofore pathological abandonment depression increasingly assumes the quality of true mourning for the lost bad objects. The stage is now set for the patient's passage from Kernberg's Stage 3 of internalized object relations to his Stage 4.

The third phase, resolution or separation, constitutes a sort of extended wrap-up of the momentous achievements of the preceding phase. The patient's capacity to mourn the lost objects, developed during the preceding phase, can now be applied to his necessary separation from the treatment staff and the milieu generally. To assist in this important termination work, a post-discharge period of outpatient treatment is usually necessary.

For optimal therapeutic results in the case of borderline and narcissistic juveniles, concomitant family treatment is a necessity. As the patient traverses the three phases of treatment, the parents accompany him on the journey. Resistance work with the parents is no less demanding and difficult than is that with the child in residence. The parents must ultimately relinquish their need to promote their child's resistance to treatment; they must reach the point at which they are able to give permission to the child to relate to, and ultimately to come to trust, the treatment staff. The parents' own middle, introjective, or working-through phase involves several sequential stages: they must also come to trust the treatment staff, condensed in their trust of their own family therapist; they must come to an understanding of how they have depersonified their child and, so far as possible, of the basis for the depersonification derived from their own blighted separation–individuation; and, as they enter into the work of the resolution or separation phase, they must proceed to healthily separate from their child as they prepare to welcome him back into their household as an appropriately self-differentiated real child, no longer the depersonified symbiont he has been for them. As a result, both parents and child are now ready to resume the mutual parent–child growth that their combined pathology had so early set awry.

MASTERSON'S THREE STAGES IN THE PSYCHOTHERAPY OF ADOLESCENT AND ADULT CASES

As expected, Masterson's (1981) account of the triphasic nature of the psychotherapeutic process with adolescents and adults with borderline personality disorder follows the foregoing sequence. The first stage encompasses what he refers to as the transformation of "transference acting-out" into "transference" as such. In the former, the patient's behavior is dominated by the projection of the components of the split object-relations unit into the therapist, accompanied by various forms of self-defeating and self-destructive behavior within and outside the therapeutic sessions. As a consequence of the therapist's persistent confrontation of such behavior, the patient comes to perceive its various manifestations as ego dystonic, and with that, the development of transference ensues. Masterson takes the latter to signify that the patient has come to perceive the therapist as a whole object, a perceptual transformation that is necessary for the patient's ability to differentiate the therapist as a "real" personage from his image of the therapist as a transference figure.

With that, interpretive transference work now becomes possible, initiating the patient's entrance into the
second stage of treatment. Now the analysis and working-
through of the underlying abandonment depression comes
to the fore. Masterson places great emphasis on the patient's ability to recognize, work through, and ultimately
subdue powerful talionic (revanchist) impulses and needs
directed toward the self, and—by displacement from the
parents—toward others (including the therapist) that are
derived from the affective components of his split object-
relations unit.

The third or termination stage of treatment consists
largely of the continuing application of the techniques
utilized during the preceding stages, now focusing particularly on the patient's ability to forego his need for exclusive
possession of the therapist from whom he must eventually
separate. As this occurs, the patient resolves his anxiety
over the possibility of functioning as a free and independent personage.

Although Masterson appears to apply this sequence of
therapeutic stages to both the borderline and the narcissistic personalities, he considers the latter to be the more
primitively developed of the two; hence, narcissistic personalities pose particular problems for treatment based on
an exceptional vulnerability to narcissistic woundings. This
view runs counter to the generally accepted concept of the
relative positions of these two major personality disorders
along the dynamic-developmental spectrum or continuum
of borderline-narcissistic personality disorders (Adler 1981,
1985, Kohut 1971, 1977, Rinsley 1980b, 1982a, 1984, 1985,
1988b, 1989). Nevertheless, his postulated sequence of

therapeutic stages accurately reflects much of the essence of what transpires during the course of treatment of border-line and narcissistic patients.

ADLER'S THREE PHASES IN THE TREATMENT OF THE BORDERLINE PERSONALITY

Adler (1985) also presents a triphasic account of the course of psychoanalytic treatment of the borderline personality. In keeping with his concept of the borderline-narcissistic personality disorder continuum (1981), he correctly views the narcissistic personality as a higher-order variant of the borderline personality, and he considers that the successful treatment of the latter causes the patient "to attain func-tions and capacities . . . similar to patients with narcissistic personality disorders" (1985, p. 86). As he points out:

> Borderline patients . . . differ from narcissistic patients in two critical respects: Their regression involves a greater degree of loss of self-cohesiveness than that experienced by the narcissistic patient, with the ultimate felt threat of annihilation . . . the basic problem for the borderline pa-tient lies in his relative lack of holding-soothing introjects— his relative incapacity to allay separation anxiety through intrapsychic resources. [p. 89]

This is in contrast to the problem of the narcissistic person-ality, whose struggle is "to maintain his tenuous sense of self-worth" (p. 89).

Accordingly, treatment during the initial phase in-

volves efforts toward the reduction and eventual elimination of the patient's all good-all bad splitting defense based
on the establishment of relatively stable holding introjects
(personified by the therapist); associated with those efforts
goes the progressive correction of distorting projections
that have intensified the negative component of the splitting. What Adler appears to be describing here is a latter-
day projection by the patient of the very young child's
grandiose self into the therapist, who thereby assumes the
quality of an *idealized parent figure*, as described by Kohut.

Phase 2 is occupied with the patient's gradual relin-
quishment of the therapist's idealized image by means of a
working-through process that Kohut (1971) terms optimal
disillusionment. If the process is successful, the patient
comes to accept the therapist's soothing-holding function
in terms of the latter's identity as a real personage, a
concerned and caring individual whose helpful ministrations are brought to bear within the professional psychotherapeutic context.

Phase 3, when successful, leads to the progressive
maturation of the patient's internalized object-relations
structures leading toward autonomous self-governance and
overall functioning. As the therapist's image becomes more
real, so too does the patient's self-image as the two increasingly differentiate from each other. As these transformations proceed, the patient's harsh, primitive superego
forerunners undergo depersonification or assimilation
(Kernberg's [1966] term for this is *metabolization*). The
resulting, more mature superego proceeds toward progressive integration with the ego, whose adaptive and coping
functions become more and more reality-oriented, hence

efficient as executors of internal regulation and as media-
tors between inner and outer experiences. These superego
forerunners, originally composed of elements of the split
object-relations unit in borderline cases and the forbid-
dingly harsh primal maternal introject in narcissistic cases,
now proceed to become integrated into an increasingly
healthy conscience. A notable degree of self-sufficiency
now develops within a context of more mature whole-
object relationships, permitting meaningful intimacy
without the terrifying prospect of fragmentation of the self
and its experiences.

PHASES OF TREATMENT ACCORDING
TO KERNBERG AND COLLEAGUES

A current monograph on the psychoanalytic psychotherapy of borderline patients by Kernberg and colleagues
(1989) provides a highly informative and detailed technical
account of the course of treatment of this group of cases.
The Kernberg group delineates an early phase, an advanced phase, and a third stage that they do not specifically
designate as a phase.

The early phase is concerned with the coalescence of
part-self and part-object representations. In their words:

[T]he important task is to transform the patient's chaotic
experiences, behaviors and interactions in the hour into a
dominant primitive object relation (and) regarding the
interpretation of the transference . . . to define the dominant object relation in the transference and, second, to

track the enactment of reciprocal roles of this object relation, again and again pointing out to the patient how the
same object relation is activated regardless of who plays
what role in their interaction. [pp. 118–119]

The significance of this early-phase work, derived from the
patient–therapist interactions during therapeutic hours,
lies in the patient's transferential exposure and projection
of his primitive, split-off self-object images (dyads) along
with their associated primitive affects; in turn, the therapist
proceeds to confront and clarify them, guided by his sensitive awareness of his often highly troubling countertransference responses to them. These self-object dyads may be
viewed as manifestations of the borderline patient's split
object-relations unit and are dealt with much as Masterson
would confront and clarify them during the resistance or
testing phase of treatment. When successful, the result of
this arduous work causes the patient to proceed to coalesce
these primitive imaginal structures into "more realistic and
balanced internal representations of the self and object"
(p. 92). Initially, these more mature representations have to
do with the patient's self-image and his image of the therapist, which now begin to generalize to other object relationships as the patient's attunement to reality grows apace.

What the Kernberg group appears to be describing as
the predominant therapeutic task of the early phase of
treatment is highly reminiscent of Masterson's concept of
the transformation of transference acting-out into transference during the resistance phase. And the concept of the
coalescence of part-self and part-object dyads is likewise
reminiscent of Adler's concept of the attenuation and

eventual elimination of the borderline patient's all good-all bad splitting and self- and object-images as a consequence of the establishment of the soothing-holding introject. As the Kernberg group shows, a prime indicator that these transformations have in fact occurred to a significant degree is the patient's ability to tolerate ambivalence (good plus bad) in contrast to his previous all good-(or)-all bad dichotomy. This means that the patient has begun the developmental journey that will carry him from Kernberg's Stage 3 toward Stage 4 of internalized object relations.

Entrance into the advanced phase of treatment begins when the patient has moved from reliance on primitive defenses (features of Kernberg's specific structural characteristics of the borderline), including splitting, projective identification, denial, omnipotence, and devaluation, toward reliance on more advanced defenses, such as repression, reaction-formation, and isolation of affect. Along with this important shift in defensive organization go other characteristics indicative of progressive psychostructural maturation: increased anxiety tolerance, increasingly effective evocative memory, and ongoing realistic remodeling of the patient's inner image of the therapist. Now, the patient reveals unmistakable evidence of a growing capacity to mourn and is increasingly able to utilize the therapist's in-depth (genetic-dynamic) interpretations to understand the pristine pathogenesis of his character pathology.

During the final period of treatment ("separation: interruptions and termination"), the essential goal is the patient's eventual separation from the therapist, accomplished by means of his now established capacity to mourn. This means, of course, that the patient has been able to accomplish much of the work of the depressive position.

The Kernberg group's description of these three sequential periods of psychoanalytic treatment is both detailed and masterful, and deserves the careful study of any clinician who works with borderline patients.

It should be pointed out, in summary, that despite often claimed differences among them, these several approaches to the understanding and treatment of borderline and narcissistic personalities are in fact strikingly similar. The stated differences generally amount to disputations over relatively minor points of theory and technique. All of them have developed a "big picture" of what is required for the treatment of these personality disorders. The ongoing dialogue among their major exponents cannot fail to add materially to an understanding of these benighted patients and how to treat them.

Chapter 19

Antisocial Types

Two contemporary clinicians, Horner (1979) and Masterson (1981), distinguish the antisocial personality from the borderline and narcissistic personalities. These are the affectionless psychopaths and psychopathic personalities presumed to be unresponsive to psychoanalytic treatment whose pervasive and overtly self-serving narcissism results from a primal failure to bond, hence to develop the early mother–infant symbiosis that is the pristine prototype for all future object relations. This view is a resurgence of the "bad seed" notion of the basically evil individual who is unable to distinguish living beings, including human beings, from inanimate objects. Their innate or inborn pathogenetic determinants are a matter of nature, not nurture.

Regarding such determinants, Esman (1980) notes that some borderline adolescents come into the world with "intrinsic deviations in the range of minimal cerebral dysfunction." Andrulonis and colleagues (1981) identify three categories of borderline adolescents and adults, which they label as nonorganic, trauma-encephalitis-epilepsy, and minimal brain dysfunction-learning disability, respectively (Andrulonis et al. 1981). Meissner (1984) considers the syndromes of minimal brain dysfunction and episodic dyscontrol as possible organic substrates to the pathogenesis of borderline personality, and Kernberg (1966) writes:

> More characteristic of the borderline personality organization may be . . . a constitutionally determined lack of anxiety tolerance interfering with the . . . synthesis of introjections of opposite valences. The most important cause of . . . borderline pathology is probably a quantitative predominance of negative introjections. Excessive negative introjections may stem both from a constitutionally determined intensity of aggressive drive derivatives and from severe early frustration. [pp. 250–251]

Numerous studies, as cited by Tucker and Pincus (1980), including the well-known longitudinal follow-up of "deviant children grown up" by Robins (1966), provide support for the concept of a heredocongenital or genetic basis for antisociality.

It would be fatuous to argue that heredocongenital determinants play no role whatever in the pathogenesis of the narcissistic characterology that typifies the antisocial personality. Their precise role, however, remains to be clarified by future research. Nevertheless, matters of nosology acquire significance in any effort to understand the relationship that the antisocial personality shares with the borderline personality and the narcissistic personality.

A great many individuals who are descriptively diagnosable as antisocial personalities (DSM-III-R) are also diagnosable as narcissistic personalities in terms of psychodynamic criteria. Kohut recognizes this clinical fact when he differentiates what he terms the dysphoric, hypersensitive, hypochondriacal *narcissistic personality disorder* and the perverse, antisocial, addictive *narcissistic behavior disorder* (Kohut 1977, Kohut and Wolf 1978), both of which share a common pathogenesis based on early failure of maternal empathy.

The narcissistic spectrum of cases encompasses a wide variety of examples of Kohut's narcissistic behavior disorder, combining features of the better-organized narcissistic personality and those of the more regression-prone, internally dysregulated borderline personality.

A prime example of such a mixed case is the late Alphonse ("Al") Capone, the infamous Chicago mobster and organized crime boss, a person of unbridled narcissistic egomania and acknowledged—if dyssocial—leadership ability, who was an unscrupulous exploiter of friend and foe alike and, who, when crossed, could become a coldblooded murderer. Bursten (1973, 1978) might classify Capone as a narcissistic personality with mixed phallic and paranoid features.

Other, more dyssocially enculturated examples would include the highest-echelon members of the Third Reich's SS, such as Adolf Eichmann and Reinhard Heydrich, who could sit calmly sipping cognac while planning the extinction of Europe's Jews, gypsies, and Jehovah's Witnesses.

Included also are sundry, often highly talented and energetic egomaniacs who populate the political arena and the entertainment, sports, and television evangelism industries and whose immense popular successes accompany personal lives replete with grossly impaired familial and wider social relationships that are often characterized by substance abuse and perverse sexuality. These are individuals whose aim is to control and enthrall others, from whom they demand endless outpourings of approbative mirroring to shore up their weakened sense of self-esteem with its underlying feelings of powerlessness and worthlessness.

Considered psychodynamically, to the extent that any given antisocial personality may also be diagnosed as a narcissistic or a borderline personality, then with appropriate application of external controls over a sufficiently lengthy period of time to preclude acting out, response to traditional psychotherapy may be expected. When in such cases therapeutic failure occurs, for which the patient's untreatability is all too often cited as the reason, two classic situations may be seen to apply: (1) failure to provide stringent-enough controls, including controls during an inpatient process, for whatever reasons, including legal strictures; (2) failure to provide stringent-enough controls for a sufficiently long period of time. Unfortunately, the traditional situation where these two conditions are ordinarily met—namely, the prison—is almost always a thoroughly antitherapeutic environment.

Are there in fact hard-core, recidivist antisocial criminals who are unable to utilize any form of proffered psychotherapy? Are there vicious, monstrously evil mentalities devoid of any trace of the milk of human kindness, who should forever be prevented from access to society, the key to whose lock-up door should be thrown away? If so, are not at least some of them the terrifying products of the intergenerational passage of defective strands of DNA and RNA, hobbled by a congenital incapacity to bond with, hence to relate to, others? Only future research will provide answers to these questions.

PART III

SUPERVISION

Who shall observe the observers?
Roman epigram

Chapter 20

Supervision and Therapy

The term *psychoanalytic treatment* defines any variety of "talking" therapy, including what is generally referred to as classical psychoanalysis, in which the major if not exclusive focus is brought to bear on the phenomena of transference and countertransference. Thus, the essence of such treatment lies in the patient's reexperiencing of earlier events, including traumatic ones, within the therapeutic or analytic process in relation to the person of the

131

therapist or analyst, and the latter's reexperiencing of such events from his own past as these are reawakened and revivified as a result of those of the patient. Kernberg (1984) differentiates psychoanalysis and psychoanalytic psychotherapy in terms of how the analyst or therapist deals with transference material as it emerges in the treatment process. Thus, in psychoanalytic psychotherapy, such material may be confronted and clarified, whereas in psychoanalysis it may be analyzed (interpreted), that is, traced back to its origins by means of the patient's use of the "basic rule" of free association, traditionally with the patient in the recumbent (couch) position. In the case of children, for whom observation of the basic rule is well-nigh impossible, the use of play replaces free association as the vehicle by which transference as well as nontransference material emerges during treatment (Klein 1932).

The fledgling analytic therapist best learns his complex and demanding craft under the tutelage and sensitive guidance of senior clinicians. This is required of the psychoanalyst-in-training by means of the use of the control case, and it is no less essential for others who seek to attain skill as psychoanalytic psychotherapists. It may be said that the prime purpose of such lengthy and often arduous apprenticeship is to assist the trainee to develop ever-greater skill in differentiating his own needs and motives from those of his patients, to not impose himself on his patients as he seeks to understand them, and to help them to help themselves. To that end, the psychoanalyst-in-training undergoes his own analysis. For the neophyte psychoanalytic psychotherapist, the supervision for his therapeutic work may, and indeed at times must, assume certain of the characteristics of a therapeutic process.

The following discussion takes up the subject of the supervision of the trainee psychotherapist's psychotherapeutic processes, in part by means of case examples and in accordance with Wolberg's (1977) general discussion of the subject.

At the outset, due note needs to be taken of that psychotherapeutic *ignis fatuus* known as the "highly motivated neurotic patient," the much sought-after ideal candidate for classical psychoanalysis. If such an individual exists at all, he rarely if ever finds his way into the office of the fledgling psychotherapist, who is almost invariably a beginning or middle-level psychiatrist resident, graduate student in clinical or counseling psychology, or graduate student in social work in fieldwork placement. These doughty trainees find themselves struggling to learn their craft with an assortment of psychotics and borderline personalities; many of the latter begin in psychotherapy while inpatients and are usually passed from one beginning psychotherapist to another as their therapist-trainees rotate from one clinical rotation to another. Not a few of them turn out to be antisocial personalities, or borderline personalities with various antisocial features, both of whom are poor candidates for expressive psychotherapeutic work. Thus, many trainees complete their general training program without the enormously important experience of having helped to bring about significant and enduring psychological change in their patients.

Note needs also to be taken of those burgeoning

"biologically oriented" psychiatric residencies whose directors and faculty regard psychodynamic concepts, and therapies based on them, as either fraudulent or, at best, irrelevant to patient care. One such program provides no supervised psychotherapeutic experience at all; the trainee must seek, find, and pay for it himself!

One trainee in such a program was told by his superviser that "talking to the patient" was a waste of time and that unless the trainee was treating the patient with psychotropic medication, he should promptly discharge him.

   Some years ago, the chief resident in a recognized psychiatric residency program told me that, upon completion of his formal residency training, he planned to move to another setting where he could enter psychoanalytic training. He said, "I had no psychotherapy training here. Most of the emphasis was on cortical evoked potentials and drugs, so I'm going to _____ , where I can learn how to do real treatment."

   Individualized psychotherapy supervision traditionally involves three personages: the patient, the therapist, and the therapist's superviser. There is thus forged a "triangle," with all the pejorative possibilities that Bowen (1978) has described in the case of dysfunctional families and their treatment. Ineffectual or even abjectly deleterious supervision, involving the three protagonists of the supervisory process, at best causes the therapy to founder and at worst proves ruinous to the patient, not to mention the therapist's training. How can this come about? A few examples follow:

   1. The therapist turns out to be a significantly disturbed individual, suffering from major psychopathology

or personality disorder, and the superviser fails to detect or react to the therapist's disturbance, hence fails to terminate the therapy and to notify the responsible member or members of the training committee that the therapist should not be permitted to engage in psychotherapeutic work under the training program's auspices. In some such cases, the would-be therapist should be counseled out of training altogether.

A young male psychiatric resident came to supervision with the case of an inpatient adolescent girl who had been diagnosed with early bipolar disorder and borderline personality disorder. During the first several months of the psychotherapy, the patient made several suicidal attempts by wrist-cutting and attempted to elope during them and at other times. From the material presented in supervision, it became clear that the therapist had been unconsciously stimulating the girl to injure herself and to run away. From these and other data, it became apparent to the superviser that the resident, an otherwise ingratiating and rather passive-aggressive man, was in fact a highly intelligent paranoid personality whose subtle injunctions to his patient to act out self-injuriously had stemmed from a pervasive lack of belief in the efficacy of hospital treatment, as well as his need to ward off feelings of sexual stimulation in response to the patient's often highly seductive posturings and communications. The superviser's efforts to assist the trainee therapist to recognize and begin to deal with his problems vis-à-vis his youthful patient fell on the deaf ears of the insightless. Accordingly, the superviser terminated the therapy, and the therapist was eventually counseled out of psychiatric training.

2. The superviser is excessively passive. Excessive superviser passivity rarely stems from incompetence as such.

Not uncommonly it results from indigenous passive or passive-aggressive personality traits in the superviser. Again, not uncommonly, it occurs in the case of supervisers who are in training to become psychoanalysts and in the case of analytically trained or informed supervisers who conduct the supervision in the fashion of the caricature of a psychoanalytic process (see pp. 153–154). In effect, by withholding advice, opinions, suggestions, and direct if gentle criticism, the superviser leaves the supervisee to fend for himself. In some such situations, the superviser's approach represents an unconscious need to compete with, vanquish, or prove oneself superior to the fledgling therapist.

A male psychiatric resident in supervision for a year for his psychotherapy process with a young, narcissistic female patient with a disabling physical deformity, switched supervisers after that period, as required by the training program. During the initial year of supervision with the original superviser, the patient had made little progress; this had evidently resulted from the prior superviser's covert and overt admonitions to the therapist that a more active and intrusive approach might disrupt the patient and, as a result, cause her to "regress." The second superviser, by contrast, took a more active approach, encouraging the therapist to explore, gently confront, clarify and, when possible, interpret transference issues and to examine his own (countertransference) responses to the material that the patient produced during the sessions. As a result, during the subsequent year the patient made notable strides in recognizing and coming to grips with early developmental issues, including her overprotective mother's fawning attitude toward her and her father's aloof avoidance of her in the face of her physical deformity. One gratifying result of this work was her growing self-esteem and a beginning conviction that she could indeed be interesting to men.

In this case, the superviser's excessively protective attitude toward the patient had significantly retarded the course of her psychotherapy by underestimating her capacity for insight and hard therapeutic work, not to mention the therapist's ability to help her to perform it. (Striking was the similarity of the superviser's essentially avoidant approach to the patient's treatment and her father's own avoidant attitude toward her; this issue was, of course, not explored with the supervisee!)

3. The superviser is excessively active and intrusive. Here, what becomes apparent is the superviser's need, in effect, to bypass the therapist and to take over the patient's treatment. As in the case of the excessively passive superviser, the excessively active and intrusive superviser manages to attempt to impose his own approach and style on the therapist to the detriment of both the psychotherapeutic and the supervisory processes.

The following is an excerpt of an informal discussion between a senior superviser and a male resident in psychiatry concerning the resident's difficulties with a psychotherapeutic case in supervision with another superviser:

S: "How do you understand the discomfort you feel in working with this patient?"

T: "Well, I think it comes from supervision."

S: "How?"

T: "Well, Dr. _____ keeps telling me to 'get in there,' to be more active and confront the patient more, and I'm uncomfortable doing that because when I try to do what he says, the patient gets very confused. I'm really afraid that directly confronting him will drive him crazy."

S: "How are you dealing with that?"

T: "Well, I go underground."

S: "What do you mean by 'underground'?"

T: "I often don't do what he tells me to do, and things go better."

S: "So you don't tell him you're ignoring his advice. Why don't you tell him and be honest about it?"

T: "Er, well, I'm afraid he'd give me a poor evaluation if he knew!"

In this case, the resident was obviously torn between his own view of what was needed in the therapy and his superviser's very different view of that, and he chose to do what he considered appropriate. Although, as it turned out, the resident's view was the correct one in this particular case, it was also evident that he was intellectually dishonestly acting out against his superviser. The impasse was resolved when the resident requested a change of supervisers, which was granted. A first order of business with the new superviser was to address the resident's proneness to subvert his prior supervision by "going underground," with gratifying results.

4. An instance of failure of the supervisee's and the superviser's personalities to match in a more general sense.

An example of such a mismatch came to light in the case of a superior, 27-year-old female resident with a liberal social outlook, and her superviser, an older senior clinician, who was an avowed conservative. The resident had started psychotherapy with a mid-twenties, dysthymic man who was also a lifelong homosexual. From the beginning, the therapist had assumed a permissive attitude toward the patient's homosexuality, believing that she should only address it if the patient agreed. In contrast, the superviser believed that the patient's homosexuality represented a symptomatic expression of underlying personality disorder that the therapist was duty-bound to address as an important aspect of the therapy. On the other hand, the therapist, not without good reason, felt that directly addressing the patient's homosexuality without clearcut evidence that the patient desired that she do so would cause the patient to terminate the therapy; she felt that the superviser was a "homophobe." Again, the male superviser considered the therapist's reluctance to face the homosexual issue with her patient constituted a resistance both to it and to the superviser, which he assumed was derived from unresolved identity issues within the therapist. The supervision reached an impasse within a few months. Accordingly, the therapist felt the need to request termination of the supervision and assignment to another superviser, and to her pleasant surprise, the superviser agreed. Another superviser was found whose social outlook more closely matched the therapist's and the therapy continued uninterrupted.

Chapter 21

Supervision as Therapy

Effective supervision, the avowed purpose of which is to enhance the supervisee's psychotherapeutic skills, invariably results in deeper accompanying changes within the supervisee (not to mention in the superviser). Accordingly, whether and to what degree the supervisory process should address such changes will determine how and to what degree it assumes the features of a therapeutic-like process.

As expected, two opposing points of view concern this important matter.

1. Supervision should rarely address issues that could subtly or otherwise transform it into a quasi-therapy, and the superviser's responsibility is to guard against such a turn of events. After all, the supervisee does not come to supervision to obtain treatment, and it is unethical for the superviser to indulge in what amounts to misplaced therapeutic zeal with an unsuspecting trainee. However, in any teaching-and-learning enterprise, and particularly within the supervisory process, transference issues related to the early parent–child relationship inevitably appear and are found to play themselves out in supervision, which consequently comes to be tinged with "therapeutic issues." To what extent should the superviser draw the supervisee's attention to them; indeed, should he do so at all?

It may also be claimed that a self-sensitive superviser who finds himself edging toward a therapeutic involvement with the supervisee, however attenuated it may be, will infer that his need to do so reflects problems within the supervisee (if not within himself) that may require some form of therapeutic intervention. Accordingly, the superviser may be expected to seek consultation with a senior colleague to assist him to recognize and resolve issues connected with his need to "treat" the supervisee, certainly before he gives serious consideration to recommending that the supervisee seek treatment elsewhere for himself.

An important training tool for supervisers is the supervisory continuous case seminar, in which qualified supervisers seek to enhance their supervisory skills in a group conducted by a senior supervising clinician. In one meeting of such a group, consisting of four superviser-participants and a senior group leader, an experienced male superviser had been presenting a supervisory process with a younger female psychiatric resident who was treating an adolescent girl in outpatient individual psychotherapy. The superviser brought a problem in supervising the resident that consisted of his discomfort in recognizing his need to coach the resident. The following interaction ensued (Pr = superviser presenting the case; P1-P3 = other superviser-participants; L = senior group leader):

L: "Tell us more about what you call 'coaching'."

Pr: "Well, I feel the need at times to tell her what to do next, even though she's doing a superb job overall."

L: "Can you talk about your feelings toward the supervisee?"

Pr: "I like her. I think well of her."

L: "Yes . . . "

Pr: "Well, I'm kind of stuck on what to say next."

P1: "I wonder if your use of the phrase 'stuck on' tells us anything."

Pr: "Oh, now I think I see. You mean I'm stuck on the trainee?"

P2: "Well, I think that P1 is implying that there may be some feelings on your part that could be connected to your need to coach her."

L: "Can you identify such feelings?"

Pr: "Hmm, yeah, I think so! Yes, I find her very attractive as well as being bright and sensitive."

L: "Does anybody else in the room want to comment on that?"

P3: "Yes, it looks like an oedipal thing."

L: "Can you explain that?"

Pr: "I think *I* can. Let me try. It seems that by my wanting to coach Dr. _____ , I'm looking at her as sort of my child, which could be my way of avoiding my attraction to her. So I could be seeing her as a sort of mixed figure, an oedipal little girl and a grown-up sexual partner."

P3: "Not to mention that she's also your supervisee!"

Pr: "Hmm, a little sadism there, P3! But I did leave that out, didn't I?"

P3: "Sorry for that!"

L: "Good, Pr! I think you're definitely on to something. So if you refrain from coaching her and leave her to do her mature thing as a colleague as well as a supervisee, she becomes a taboo would-be lover for you."

Pr: "Yes, I see that clearly now."

P2: "OK, so don't infantilize her. Let her do her good job with her patient with a minimum of telling her what to do."

The foregoing interpretive interactions proved sufficient to help the superviser to desist from his efforts to coach his supervisee, with salutary results for both the therapeutic and the supervisory processes. In this case, the superviser's seminar served the needs of the resident's supervision by freeing the superviser to modify his approach to the supervisee without the necessity to introduce transference and countertransference issues into the supervision.

2. Therapeutic issues have a legitimate place within the supervisory process, depending on the superviser's perspicacity and diplomacy and the supervisee's capacity to make use of them without causing disruption to the therapy or deleterious pesonal effects in the supervisee. In such cases, it is assumed that the superviser's approach to the supervisee is essentially devoid of contaminating countertransference determinants; these, when present, are usually found to represent displaced parental needs with grandiose, narcissistic overtones, including envy of the supervisee,

jealousy of the supervisee's relationship with the patient, and competitiveness derived from oedipal and related sibling rivalry needs.

An example of the propriety of introducing therapeutic issues into psychotherapy supervision is illustrated in the case of a young male psychiatric resident who had been treating a middle-aged professional man with narcissistic personality disorder; the patient had been discharged from inpatient treatment for an episode of major depression during which he had made a suicidal attempt by attempting to asphyxiate himself via automobile exhaust, only to abort the attempt by turning off the engine and departing the vehicle when he felt drowsy. After several months of supervision for the twice-weekly psychotherapeutic process, it became evident that the therapist had been permitting the patient to drone on and on during the sessions in a seemingly endless series of essentially vapid, verbosely circumstantial intellectualizations. Underlying these could be noted the patient's need to totally control the sessions, to ward off any potential impact the therapy might have on him. Despite repeated, gentle suggestions by the superviser that the therapist more actively focus on the patient's need to thus ward him off, the therapist abjectly failed to do so.

The supervisee was finally able to tell the superviser that he feared that even gentle efforts to take charge, to "push" the patient, might precipitate another suicidal attempt by the patient. Information gleaned from the supervisee's other supervisers now clearly indicated that the supervisee had been unduly passive and noninterventive in his interactions with other patients, both in psychotherapy and in his management of inpatient cases for whose overall treatment he was responsible.

The superviser now took up the problem of inappropriate passivity with the supervisee. The latter freely and with not a little insight acknowledged his problem with taking charge, and he proceeded to relate it to a longstanding pattern of interactions with others that he ascribed to an inordinately strict upbringing. He averred, "My parents were rigidly religious people who never praised me for anything I did. It was unacceptable to be aggressive, and as far back as I can remember whenever I was, my father would sit me down and lecture for hours from the Bible." He could agree, with some sense of relief, that this pattern was a deeply ingrained characterologic feature that he felt powerless to change, and he was able to accept a recommendation that he undergo evaluation for analytic treatment. Subsequently, he was accepted for analytic psychotherapy and remained in and eventually completed his training.

Chapter 22

Supervisee Treatment

Recommending or requiring that a psychotherapy supervisee seek and obtain psychotherapy for himself constitutes one of the most formidable issues with which the superviser must contend. When it is made, it results from either of two major circumstances. Either the supervisee is deemed psychologically disturbed or otherwise inept enough to warrant the termination of his psychotherapeutic work as such, or his continuation as a psychotherapist is made contingent on his seeking and obtaining treatment for himself. In some of the former cases, as noted, the trainee may be counseled out of further mental health training altogether.

Although the question may well be raised concerning how it came to pass that a significantly disturbed or inept supervisee got as far as he did in beginning to perform supervised psychotherapy, the fact remains that such a situation is by no means rare. However it manages to occur, major psychopathological or characterologic problems that emerge in the trainee are especially prone to reveal themselves in supervision when the trainee begins to work with patients with borderline and narcissistic personality disorders.

A very different situation arises when the otherwise competent or even superior trainee is already undergoing psychotherapy or psychoanalysis on his own. In such situations, the supervision and the supervisee's own treatment constitute parallel processes. But whether voluntarily engaged in or required, the supervisee's treatment often poses significant problems for his supervision in managing to set covert or overt limits on the extent to which the superviser may feel free to deal with therapeutic issues within the supervision. One problem for supervision arises when the supervisee quite naturally, and without any attempt at concealment, takes material to his therapy or analysis without bringing it into his supervision, where it needs to be aired. This displaced material often includes patient-related issues as well as significant supervisory transference issues of which the superviser needs to be aware. In my experience, whatever the nature of the displaced material, a totally "hands off" attitude on the superviser's part toward therapeutic issues as they emerge during supervision may significantly interfere with the trainee's learning process. Furthermore, no superviser is in a position to deal with any issues or material if they are diverted into the supervisee's own treatment and consequently never appear during supervision.

This knotty problem involving parallel psychotherapeutic and supervisory processes cannot be effectively approached and resolved by means of semi-rigid or inflexible rules governing the superviser's approach to the supervisee and the issues that the latter brings or does not bring into the supervision. Here, as elsewhere in the complex teaching and learning experience, basic ethics require full respect for the supervisee's own treatment, while not ignoring matters of a more personal nature that emerge during supervision. No reasonably psychologically healthy trainee will make serious, conscious, or less than fully conscious attempts to split and divide the two processes. Rather, therapeutic issues that appear in the course of supervision are grist for the trainee's own therapeutic mill, as it were, and attention to them will not subvert the latter.

A different aspect of the matter of therapeutic issues in psychotherapy supervision has to do with the supervisee who appears to attempt to convert the supervision into a therapeutic process by directly and frequently contaminating the supervision with personal matters, which on their face appear to the superviser to be inappropriate to the supervisory process. Here again, the question arises concerning how the superviser should best deal with this situation. One stock answer is that when the supervisee indulges in this practice, he is almost directly asking for treatment, and the superviser should therefore, and with no little dispatch, recommend it or even attempt to motivate the training program to enforce it under penalty of discontinuing the supervisee's training. A major consideration here has to do with whether the supervisee's "contamination" of the supervision with personal matters occurs within a context of marginal or inadequate psychotherapeutic performance, and furthermore, to what extent the superviser is able to judge that the contamination has actually significantly impeded or even vitiated the supervision.

An older, divorced female child psychiatry fellow was treating a 5-year-old girl in thrice-weekly analytic psychotherapy, predominantly utilizing play technique. Numerous themes appeared in the child's play, centering on enormous greed, omnipotence, mistrust, and guilt based on powerful destructive impulses toward the therapist, during the early weeks of therapy. The supervisee dealt with these with appropriate confrontation and clarification, interspersed with which were numerous brief periods in which she properly physically restrained the young child from acting destructively toward her and toward the toys and office furnishings.

At about the time the beginnings of a therapeutic alliance could be noted, reflected in part in the child's growing trust in the therapist and in a disappearance of the child's aggressive acting-in episodes, the supervisee began to introduce topics into the supervisory hours related to her early life experiences. These generally took the form of increasingly extended statements concerning her parents and siblings and her own failed and childless marriage. Because the superviser believed that bringing this material into the supervision had not yet impaired its functioning, it was suggested to the supervisee that its appearance during supervision could be reflecting her responses to the material that the patient's play, general behavior, and verbal communications were bringing into therapy. This was brought to a focus, and the following dialogue ensued:

T: "I feel a little put out with myself that I've been talking about myself so much. I didn't realize I was."

S: "It's all right. You've done nothing to be censured for, but I think we need to look at it."

T: "Yes."

S: "Go ahead."

T: "Er, I'm really at a loss to know where to start. Can you help me a little?"

S: "It occurred to me that you began to discuss personal and family issues at about the time you achieved some success in developing an alliance with the youngster."

T: "Hmm, I can confirm that. It was around the time you and I both came to the conclusion that the therapy was beginning to 'take off,' wasn't it?"

S: "Yes, it was. Do you have any further thoughts about that?"

T: "Well, I'm not sure. No, wait, I think I do! That's about the time I really began to like M_____ . It's when I started to call her by her first name, and I felt she was really warming up to me."

S: "And . . . ?"

T: "And I was warming up to her."

S: "Any further clues?"

T: "Hmm, no. Wait a minute! My liking M_____ more and talking about myself more in here . . . could it be that I began to see my relationship with M_____ less as therapy and more on a personal basis?"

S: "I think you're on to something, Dr. _____ ."

T: "But I'm still in the dark about the connection."

S: "Well, I suspect that really getting to like M_____ brought out some maternal feelings."

T: "Ah, let me think a minute. Yes, I began to feel like her mother, so I transferred that to you, and I began to relate to you as if you could be my father. Hmm, very interesting!"

S: "Good, so now I'll act like a benevolent father and tell you you've done a good job in putting that together."

T: "With a little help from you, dad!"

Chapter 23

Other Supervisory Pitfalls

In addition to the foregoing, several other problems associated with supervision readily come to mind.

SUPERVISION AS A CARICATURE OF PSYCHOANALYSIS

An extreme variant of supervision conducted by an excessively passive superviser, this form of supervision, not rarely carried out by supervisors who are themselves in psychoanalytic training, is also conducted by others who are devoted to the long discredited myth that the analyst, therapist, or supervisor should serve as a "blank screen" (see Voth 1972). In such cases, the hapless supervisee is left with little more than retorted queries ("What do you think about that?") or even muteness.

The comments of a psychiatric resident to his new superviser are relevant here. In response to the latter's question concerning how his prior supervision for an adolescent's psychotherapy had been, he replied, "Well, I was irritated most of the time. Dr. _____ practically never opened his mouth. He just sat there, and when I would ask him a question he'd mutter something like "Ah" or "Hmm," and once in a rare while I'd get, "What do you think?" The kid was all over the place and much of the time I didn't know what was going on or what I should be doing!" (Did you learn anything from that?) "Well, I guess I did. After all, nothing's a total waste!" (What was that?) "Well, how not to do supervision!"

The assumption underlying this sort of supervision holds that any effort by the therapist to take charge or to take control of the therapeutic process, to limit or preclude the patient's acting in, will somehow limit or preclude the patient's expression of important material. As noted before, however, such behavior on the therapist's part, especially with children, adolescents, and impulsive, action-oriented borderline and some narcissistic personalities, often has the opposite effect. Of course, the same holds true in the case of the supervisory process.

AVOIDANCE OF SEXUAL MATERIAL

There is among some supervisers the view that sexual or sexually related material is "too hot to handle" by the

beginning psychotherapist, particularly when the therapist–patient dyad is of differing genders, and most notably
when a younger male trainee is treating a young female
patient.

A case in point involved an unmarried, depressed woman in her
late twenties, an undergraduate college student, who had been
born with a congenital paralysis of both lower extremities, and
who had an automatic bladder and an enterostomy, who was in
individual psychotherapy with an older, married male psychiatric resident. The psychotherapy, which had been supervised for approximately a year, had amounted to little more
than a supportive, reality-oriented process in which confrontation had been held to a minimum and interpretive work
eschewed.

Shortly after a new superviser entered the case, it became
abundantly evident that key transference issues had been pree-
ruptively lurking beneath the superficial exchanges between the
patient and her therapist. It also appeared that the patient
possessed enough ego strength to be able to deal with them with
the therapist's careful guidance. Accordingly, over the next year,
transference issues came to increasing focus in the therapeutic
sessions, and the therapist's countertransference responses came
to a focus within the supervision. Early attention to the patient's
sexual and paternal–parental fantasies toward the therapist
yielded a rich harvest of long-repressed and long-suppressed
material from the patient, centering on her sexual preoccupation
and frustration; her impotent rage over her deformity and its
effects in blighting her relationships; her fear that no intimate
relationships would ever be possible for her; and her deeply
depressive chagrin regarding her inability to achieve orgasm in
masturbation. With respect to the last of these, the therapist's
superviser assisted him in becoming comfortable with assuming
a more didactic, instructional role, including providing the-

patient with acceptable, medically based reading material devoted to sexual hygiene and functions, to which she responded with healthy fervor.

An important result of this work was the emergence of long-repressed material from the patient concerning frequent experiences of sexual abuse by her older brother during her elementary school years, against which she could not defend herself in view of her immobility. As her repressed rage related to these experiences surfaced during her therapy hours, the patient's depression proceeded to remit.

The therapy could now begin to address the reality issues that had been the almost sole prior focus of the patient's treatment.

It goes without saying that great care and sensitivity are essential for the neophyte therapist in dealing with sexual material, and a major aspect of effective supervision concerns providing guidance in assisting the therapist to develop a sense of personal comfort in approaching it.

AVOIDANCE AND SUPPRESSION OF PSYCHOTIC MATERIAL

It is very difficult for a therapist to retain one's composure in the face of wildly disorganized, or subtly or grossly thought-disordered communications from one's psychotherapy patient. Such material, however, is the order of the day among borderline personalities undergoing micropsychotic episodes. It is often said that, under such circumstances, the therapist should at least acknowledge such material, and then attempt to suppress it and redirect the patient toward realistic topics; this approach, however, does not necessarily bear therapeutic fruit, as it were. Two examples of contrasting approaches to such material, taken out of context, will be illustrative:

Example 1 (a borderline patient, with features of a paranoid personality):

P: "I hope you'll vote for me when I run for governor."

T: "Umm, Mr. B_____ , it's okay to tell me that, but don't tell anybody else."

P: "Yeah, I know, that's what everybody tells me—shut up!"

T: "I'm not telling you to shut up. You can tell *me*."

P: "Yes you are! You're telling me to shut up because you don't want to hear it either!"

Example 2 (a schizophrenic patient who, when reasonably well compensated, presents the appearance of a borderline personality with antisocial features):

P: "Today I am a camel."

T: "What kind—Bactrian or dromedary?"

P: "You know the difference?"

T: "Sure I do."

P: "Bactrian."

T: "So you have two humps and not just one."

P: "Right! I have two humps so I can carry more food and water. You know—the ship of the desert. I can go much further than anything else."

T: "So you can make it in a difficult, hostile environment."

P: "I'm really glad you know that 'cause I know it too!"

T: "Right!"

P: "So I'm not a total mess."

T: "Right! I knew we could agree on something."

Note that in this example, the supervisee therapist's careful and respectful attention to the patient's bizarre opening statement brought about a more realistic exchange between them and opened up an important communication from the patient concerning how he felt about himself. The therapist later told his superviser, "It was serendipity. It was a lucky thing that I happened to know something about camels," to which the superviser replied, "Yes, and you also knew how to use what you knew."

CONFIDENTIALITY AND SUPERVISED PSYCHOTHERAPY

Whatever transpires during a formal psychotherapeutic process is protected by limited privilege in a majority of jurisdictions. However, the law sanctions what would otherwise constitute breach of confidentiality in the case of peer review and for the purposes of legitimate training supervision (Slovenko 1980). "Confidentiality as an absolute principle would impede the 'quality control' of care. . . . Supervision in training . . . calls for disclosure of information about the patient" (Slovenko and Grossman 1988, p. 11).

Thus, a patient receiving supervised psychotherapy will ordinarily have no cause of action against the therapist or the therapist's superviser merely by virtue of the fact that the psychotherapy is supervised. Whether or not to inform a psychotherapy patient that material from the psychotherapy sessions will be shared with a third-party superviser comes down to a consideration of the issues of the particular case and not to a matter of law. Again, different supervisors view the matter differently.

Ideally, whether or not to inform the patient concerning the supervision should be discussed between the
superviser and the supervisee prior to the inception of the
therapeutic contract and the beginning of the therapy. In
my experience, no hard and fast rule applies here. In some
cases, it is in the best interest of the patient and of the
therapeutic process to inform the patient beforehand,
whereas in others, it is better not to do so. The most
frequently cited reason for not informing the patient derives from the not unapposite view that to do so invariably
"triangulates" the therapy, splitting the patient's transference between the therapist and the supervisor's shadowy
figure lurking in the background. It cannot be denied that,
in some cases at least, the patient will develop a view of the
therapist as something less than a fully competent and
knowledgeable figure whose attitudes and communications
in the therapy are dictated by a hidden, more competent
other.

An egregious example of such a situation occurred during the
course of a psychiatric resident's individual psychotherapy of a
narcissistic, middle-aged man. Unbeknownst to the superviser,
the resident from time to time would say to the patient, "I'll have
to ask my superviser about that." During one session, the
disgusted patient finally blurted out, "I don't think you know
what you're doing! If you have to ask your superviser all the time,
why don't I just talk to him instead of you!" Needless to say, the
psychotherapy foundered.

The teaching and learning of psychoanalytic treatment is a demanding endeavor for supervisee and superviser alike. Ultimately, the sharpening and deepening of

the trainee's skills are accompanied by a concomitant
growth of his or her maturity and sagacity as a person. The
same may be said of the sharpening and deepening of the
superviser's skills both as superviser and as therapist or
analyst himself. And the supervised psychotherapeutic process is a major crucible in which such felicitous shared
growth comes to pass.

References

Abelin, E. L. (1971a). *Esquisse d'une Théorie Etiopathogé-nique Unifiée des Schizophrénies*. Bern: Hans Huber.

_____ (1971b). The role of the father in the separation-individuation process. In: *Separation-Individuation*, ed. J. B. McDevitt and C. F. Settlage, pp. 229–252. New York: International Universities Press.

_____ (1975). Some further observations and comments on the earliest role of the father. *International Journal of Psycho-Analysis* 56:293–302.

161

_____ (1980). Triangulation, the role of the father and the origins of core gender identity during the rapprochement subphase. In: *Rapprochement: The Critical Subphase of Separation-Individuation*, ed. R. F. Lax, S. Bach, and J. A. Burland, pp. 151–169. New York: Jason Aronson.

Adler, G. (1981). The borderline-narcissistic personality disorder continuum. *American Journal of Psychiatry* 138:46–50.

_____ (1985). *Borderline Psychopathology and Its Treatment*. New York: Jason Aronson.

Akhtar, S., and Thomson, J. A. (1982). Overview: Narcissistic personality disorder. *American Journal of Psychiatry* 139: 12–20.

Aldrich, C. K. (1987). Acting out and acting up: The superego lacuna revisited. *American Journal of Orthopsychiatry* 57:402–406.

Andrulonis, P. A., Glueck, B. C., Stroebel, C. F., Vogel, N. G., Shapiro, A. L., and Aldridge, D. M. (1981). Organic brain dysfunction and the borderline syndrome. *Psychiatric Clinics of North America* 4:47–66.

Balint, M. (1968). *The Basic Fault: Therapeutic Aspects of Regression*. London: Tavistock.

Beres, D. (1968). The humanness of human beings: Psychoanalytic considerations. *Psychoanalytic Quarterly* 37:487–522.

Bernstein, A. E., and Walker, G. M. (1981). *An Introduction to Contemporary Psychoanalysis*. New York: Jason Aronson.

Bibring, E. (1953). The mechanism of depression. In: *Affective Disorders*, ed. P. Greenacre, pp. 13–48. New York: International Universities Press.

Bion, W. R. (1967). *Second Thoughts: Selected Papers on Psychoanalysis*. New York: Jason Aronson.

Bleiberg, E. (1987). Stages in the treatment of narcissistic children and adolescents. *Bulletin of the Menninger Clinic* 51:296–313.

———— (1988a). Developmental pathogenesis of narcissistic disorders in children. *Bulletin of the Menninger Clinic* 52:3–15.

———— (1988b). Adolescence, sense of self, and narcissistic vulnerability. *Bulletin of the Menninger Clinic* 52:211–228.

Bowen, M. (1978). *Family Therapy in Clinical Practice.* New York: Jason Aronson.

Bowlby, J. (1953). Some pathological processes set in train by early mother–child separation. *Journal of Mental Science* 99:265–272.

———— (1960a). Grief and mourning in infancy and early childhood. *Psychoanalytic Study of the Child* 15:9–52.

———— (1960b). Separation anxiety. *International Journal of Psycho-Analysis* 41:89–113.

———— (1962). Childhood bereavement and psychiatric illness. In: *Aspects of Psychiatric Research*, ed. D. Richter, J. M. Tanner, L. Taylor, and O. L. Zangwill, pp. 262–293. London: Oxford University Press.

Braun, B. G. (1984). Towards a theory of multiple personality and other dissociative phenomena. *Psychiatric Clinics of North America.*

Bursten, B. (1973). Some narcissistic personality types. *International Journal of Psycho-Analysis* 54:287–300.

———— (1978). A diagnostic framework. *International Review of Psycho-Analysis* 5:15–31.

Clary, W. F. (1984). Multiple personality and borderline personality. *Psychiatric Clinics of North America.*

Danielian, J., and Lister, E. D. (1988). The negative therapeutic reaction: The uses of negation. *Journal of the American Academy of Psychoanalysis* 16:431–450.

DSM-III-R (1987). *Diagnostic and Statistical Manual of Mental Disorders*, 3rd ed.-rev. Washington, DC: American Psychiatric Association.

Ekstein, R., and Friedman, S. W. (1957). The function of acting out, play action and play acting in the psychotherapeutic process. *Journal of the American Psychoanalytic Association* 5:581–629.

Erikson, E. H. (1963). *Childhood and Society*. Rev. ed. New York: Norton.

Esman, A. H. (1980). Adolescent psychopathology and the rapprochement process. In: *Rapprochement: The Critical Subphase of Separation-Indviduation*, ed. R. F. Lax, S. Bach, and J. A. Burland, pp. 285–297. New York: Jason Aronson.

Eysenck, H. J. (1967). *The Biological Basis of Personality*. Springfield, IL: Charles C Thomas.

Fairbairn, W. R. D. (1941). A revised psychopathology of the psychoses and psychoneuroses. In: *An Object-Relations Theory of the Personality*, pp. 28–58. New York: Basic Books, 1954.

––––––– (1944). Endopsychic structure considered in terms of object relationships (with 1951 *Addendum*). In: *An Object-Relations Theory of the Personality*, pp. 82–136. New York: Basic Books, 1954.

––––––– (1954). *An Object-Relations Theory of the Personality*. New York: Basic Books.

Federn, P. (1952). *Ego Psychology and the Psychoses*. Ed. P. Weiss. New York: Basic Books.

Fenichel, O. (1945). *The Psychoanalytic Theory of Neurosis*. New York: Norton.

Ferenczi, S. (1919). *Further Contributions to the Theory and Technique of Psychoanalysis*. Ed. J. Rickman. Trans. T. I. Suttie. London: Hogarth Press, 1950.

Fraiberg, S. (1969). Libidinal object constancy and mental representation. *Psychoanalytic Study of the Child* 24:9–47.

Freud, A. (1960). Discussion of Dr. John Bowlby's paper. *Psychoanalytic Study of the Child* 15:53–62.

———— (1966). Obsessional neurosis: A summary of psychoanalytic views. *International Journal of Psycho-Analysis* 47: 116–122.

———— (1968). Panel discussion held at the 25th Congress of the International Psycho-Analytical Association, Copenhagen, July 1987. *International Journal of Psycho Analysis* 49:506–512.

Freud, S. (1905). Fragment of an analysis of a case of hysteria. *Standard Edition* 7:7–122, 1953.

———— (1913a). The disposition to obsessional neurosis. *Standard Edition*, 12:313–326, 1958.

———— (1913b). On beginning the treatment (further recommendations on the technique of psycho-analysis I). *Standard Edition* 12:123, 1958.

———— (1914a). On narcissism: An introduction. *Standard Edition* 14:73–102, 1957.

———— (1914b). Remembering, repeating, and working through-(further recommendations on the technique of psycho-analysis II). *Standard Edition* 12:147–156.

———— (1916). Some character types met with in psycho-analytic work. *Standard Edition* 14:311–333.

———— (1917). Mourning and melancholia. *Standard Edition* 14:243–258, 1957

Frosch, J. (1960). Psychotic character. *Journal of the American Psychoanalytic Association* 8:544–551.

———— (1964). The psychotic character: clinical psychiatric considerations. *Psychiatric Quarterly* 38:81–96.

———— (1970). Psychoanalytic considerations of the psychotic character. *Journal of the American Psychoanalytic Association* 18:24–50.

Goldstein, K. (1939). *The Organism: A Holistic Approach to Biology*. New York: American Book Company.

———— (1959). Functional disturbances in brain damage. In:

American Handbook of Psychiatry, ed. S. Arieti, vol. 1, pp. 770–794. New York: Basic Books.

Greenberg, J. R., and Mitchell, S. A. (1983). *Object Relations in Psychoanalytic Theory*. Cambridge, MA: Harvard University Press.

Grinker, R. R., Werble, B., and Drye, R. (1968). *The Borderline Syndrome: A Behavioral Study of Ego Functions*. New York: Basic Books.

Grinker, R. R., and Werble, B. (1977). *The Borderline Patient*. New York: Jason Aronson.

Grosskurth, P. (1987). *Melanie Klein: Her World and Her Work*. Cambridge, MA: Harvard University Press.

Grotstein, J. S. (1981). *Splitting and Projective Identification*. New York: Jason Aronson.

Hartmann, H. (1939). *Ego Psychology and the Problem of Adaptation*. New York: International Universities Press.

———— (1952). The mutual influences in the development of ego and id. In: *Essays on Ego Psychology*, pp. 155–182. New York: International Universities Press, 1964.

———— (1956a). The development of the ego concept in Freud's work. In: *Essays on Ego Psychology*, pp. 268–296. New York: International Universities Press, 1964.

———— (1956b). Notes on the reality principle. In: *Essays on Ego Psychology*, pp. 241–267. New York: International Universities Press, 1964.

Hedges, L. (1983). *Listening Perspectives in Psychotherapy*. New York: Jason Aronson.

Horner, A. J. (1979), *Object Relations and the Developing Ego in Therapy*. New York: Jason Aronson.

Jacobson, E. (1964). *The Self and the Object World*. New York: International Universities Press.

Kernberg, O. F. (1966). Structural derivatives of object relationships. *International Journal of Psycho-Analysis* 47:236–253.

———— (1970). Factors in the psychoanalytic treatment of narcissistic personalities. *Journal of the American Psychoanalytic Association* 18:51–85.

———— (1972). Early ego integration and object relations. *Annals of the New York Academy of Sciences* 193:233–247.

———— (1975). *Borderline Conditions and Pathological Narcissism.* New York: Jason Aronson.

———— (1977). The structural diagnosis of borderline personality. In *Borderline Personality Disorders: The Concept, The Syndrome, The Patient,* ed. P. Hartocollis, pp. 87–121. New York: International Universities Press.

———— (1980). *Internal World and External Reality: Object Relations Theory Applied.* New York: Jason Aronson.

———— Kernberg, O. F. (1982a). The psychotherapeutic treatment of borderline personalities. In: *Psychiatry 1982: The American Psychiatric Association Annual Review,* ed. L. Grinspoon, pp. 470–487. Washington, DC: American Psychiatric Press.

———— (1982b). Supportive psychotherapy with borderline conditions. In: *Critical Problems in Psychiatry,* ed. J. O. Cavenar, Jr., and H. K. H. Brodie, pp. 180–202. Philadelphia: Lippincott.

———— (1984). *Severe Personality Disorders: Psychotherapeutic Strategies.* New Haven: Yale University Press.

Kernberg, O. F., Selzer, M. A., Koenigsberg, H. W., Carr, A. C., and Appelbaum, A. H. (1989). *Psychodynamic Psychotherapy of Borderline Patients.* New York: Basic Books.

Klein, M. (1932). *The Psycho-Analysis of Children.* London: Hogarth Press.

———— (1935). A contribution to the psychogenesis of manic-depressive states. In: *Melanie Klein: Love, Guilt and Reparation & Other Works, 1921–1945,* pp. 262–289. New York: Delacorte Press, 1975.

_____ (1940). Mourning and its relation to manic-depressive states. In: *Melanie Klein: Love, Guilt and Reparation & Other Works, 1921–1945*, pp. 344–369. New York: Delacorte Press, 1975.

_____ (1945). The Oedipus complex in the light of early anxieties. In: *Melanie Klein: Love, Guilt and Reparation & Other Works, 1921–1945*, pp. 370–419. New York: Delacorte Press, 1975.

_____ (1946). Notes on some schizoid mechanisms. In: *Melanie Klein: Envy and Gratitude & Other Works, 1946–1963*, pp. 1–24. New York: Delacorte Press, 1975.

_____ (1948). On the theory of anxiety and guilt. In: *Melanie Klein: Envy and Gratitude & Other Works, 1946–1963*, pp. 25–42. New York: Delacorte Press, 1975.

_____ (1952). Some theoretical conclusions regarding the emotional life of the infant. In: *Melanie Klein: Envy and Gratitude & Other Works, 1946–1963*, pp. 61–93. New York: Delacorte Press, 1975.

_____ (1957). *Envy and gratitude*. In: *Melanie Klein: Envy and Gratitude & Other Works, 1946–1963*, pp. 176–235. New York: Delacorte Press, 1975.

_____ (1963). On the sense of loneliness. In: *Melanie Klein: Envy and Gratitude & Other Works, 1946–1963*, pp. 300–313. New York: Delacorte Press, 1975.

Kohut, H. (1971). *The Analysis of the Self: A Systematic Approach to the Psychoanalytic Treatment of Narcissistic Personality Disorders.* The Psychoanalytic Study of the Child Monograph No. 4. New York: International Universities Press.

_____ (1977). *The Restoration of the Self.* New York: International Universities Press.

Kohut, H., and Wolf, E. S. (1978). The disorders of the self and their treatment: An outline. *International Journal of Psycho-Analysis* 59:413–425.

Kulish, N. (1988). Precocious ego development and obsessive compulsive neurosis. *Journal of the American Academy of Psychoanalysis* 16:167–187.

Kut Rosenfeld, S. K., and Sprince, M. P. (1963). An attempt to formulate the meaning of the concept "borderline." *Psychoanalytic Study of the Child* 18:603–635.

Lacan, J. (1949). Le stade du miroir comme formateur de la fonction du Je. *Revue Francaise de Psychanalyse* 4:449–455. (Cf: Benvenuto, B., and Kennedy, R., *The Works of Jacques Lacan: An Introduction.* New York: St. Martin's Press, 1986, pp. 47–62).

Lewis, J. M. (1970). The development of an adolescent inpatient service. *Adolescence* 5:303–312.

Mahler, M. S. (1965). On early infantile psychosis: The symbiotic and autistic syndromes. *Journal of the American Academy of Child Psychiatry* 4:554–568. Reprinted in: *The Selected Papers of Margaret S. Mahler,* vol. 1, pp. 155–168. New York: Jason Aronson, 1979.

———— (1968). *On Human Symbiosis and the Vicissitudes of Individuation, Vol. 1: Infantile Psychosis.* In collaboration with M. Furer. New York: International Universities Press.

———— (1971). A study of the separation-individuation process and its possible application to borderline phenomena in the psychoanalytic situation. *Psychoanalytic Study of the Child* 26:403–424. Reprinted in: *The Selected Papers of Margaret S. Mahler,* vol. 2, pp. 169–187. New York: Jason Aronson, 1979.

Mahler, M. S., Pine, F., and Bergman, A. (1975). *The Psychological Birth of the Human Infant: Symbiosis and Individuation.* New York: Basic Books.

Malin, A., and Grotstein, J. S. (1966). Projective identification in the therapeutic process. *International Journal of Psycho-Analysis* 47:26–31.

Masterson, J. F. (1967). *The Psychiatric Dilemma of Adolescence.* Boston: Little Brown.

_____ (1971). Treatment of the adolescent with borderline syndrome. *Bulletin of the Menninger Clinic* 35:5–18.

_____ (1972). *Treatment of the Borderline Adolescent: A Developmental Approach.* New York: Wiley-Interscience.

_____ (1974). Intensive psychotherapy of the adolescent with a borderline syndrome. In: *American Handbook of Psychiatry,* ed. S. Arieti, 2nd ed. vol. 2, pp. 250–263. New York: Basic Books.

_____ (1976). *Psychotherapy of the Borderline Adult: A Developmental Approach.* New York: Brunner/Mazel.

_____ (1981). *The Narcissistic and Borderline Disorders: An Integrated Developmental Approach.* New York: Brunner/Mazel.

Masterson, J. F., and Rinsley, D. B. (1975). The borderline syndrome: The role of the mother in the genesis and psychic structure of the borderline personality. *International Journal of Psycho-Analysis* 56:163–177.

McArthur, D. S. (1988). *Birth of a Self in Adulthood.* Northvale, NJ: Jason Aronson.

Meissner, W. W. (1984). *The Borderline Spectrum: Differential Diagnosis and Developmental Issues.* New York: Jason Aronson.

_____ (1988). *Treatment of Patients in the Borderline Spectrum.* Northvale, NJ: Jason Aronson.

Metcalf, D. R., and Spitz, R. A. (1978). The transitional object: Critical developmental period and organizer of the psyche. In: *Between Reality and Fantasy: Transitional Objects and Phenomena,* ed. A. Grolnick, and L. Barkin, in collaboration with W. Muensterberger, pp. 99–108. New York: Jason Aronson.

Milner, M. (1969). *The Hands of the Living God: An Account of a*

Psychoanalytic Treatment. New York: International Universities Press.

Modell, A. (1968). *Object Love and Reality: An Introduction to a Psychoanalytic Theory of Object Relations.* New York: International Universities Press.

———— (1984). *Psychoanalysis in a New Context.* New York: International Universities Press.

Morrison, A. P. (1983). Shame, ideal self, and narcissism. *Contemporary Psychoanalysis* 19:295–318.

Nagera, H. (1966). Sleep and its disturbances approached developmentally. *Psychoanalytic Study of the Child* 21: 393–447.

Offer, D. (1967). Normal adolescents: Interview strategy and selected results. *Archives of General Psychiatry* 17:285–290.

Offer, D., Sabshin, M., and Marcus, D. (1965). Clinical evaluation of normal adolescents. *American Journal of Psychiatry* 121:864–872.

Piaget, J. (1937). *The Construction of Reality in the Child.* Trans. M. Cook. New York: Basic Books, 1954.

Rado, S. (1928). The problem of melancholia. *International Journal of Psycho-Analysis* 9:420–438.

Redl, F. (1959a). Strategy and technique of the life space interview. *American Journal of Orthopsychiatry* 29:1–18.

———— (1959b). The concept of a "therapeutic milieu." *American Journal of Orthopsychiatry* 29:721–736.

Rexford, E. N. (1978). *A Developmental Approach to Problems of Acting Out.* Rev. ed. New York: International Universities Press.

Rinsley, D. B. (1971). The adolescent inpatient: Patterns of depersonification. *Psychiatric Quarterly* 45:3–22.

———— (1979). Fairbairn's object-relations theory: A reconsideration in terms of newer knowledge. *Bulletin of the Menninger Clinic* 43:489–514.

_____ (1980a). *Treatment of the Severely Disturbed Adolescent.* New York: Jason Aronson.

_____ (1980b). The developmental etiology of borderline and narcissistic disorders. *Bulletin of the Menninger Clinic* 44:127–134.

_____ (1980c). Diagnosis and treatment of borderline and narcissistic children and adolescents. *Bulletin of the Menninger Clinic.* 44:147–170.

_____ (1980d). Principles of therapeutic milieu with children. In: *Emotional Disorders in Children and Adolescents: Medical and Psychological Approaches to Treatment,* ed. G. P. Sholevar, R. M. Benson, and B. J. Blinder, pp. 191–208. New York: SP Medical and Scientific Books.

_____ (1982a). *Borderline and Other Self Disorders: A Developmental and Object-Relations Perspective.* New York: Jason Aronson.

_____ (1982b). Object relations theory and psychotherapy, with particular reference to the self-disordered patient. In: *Technical Problems in the Treatment of the Severely Disturbed Patient,* ed. P. L. Giovacchini and L. B. Boyer, pp. 187–213. New York: Jason Aronson.

_____ (1982c). Fairbairn's object relations and classical concepts of dynamics and structure. In: *Borderline and Other Self Disorders: A Developmental and Object-Relations Perspective,* pp. 251–270. New York: Jason Aronson.

_____ (1984). A comparison of borderline and narcissistic personality disorders. *Bulletin of the Menninger Clinic* 48:1–9.

_____ (1985). Notes on the pathogenesis and nosology of borderline and narcissistic personality disorders. *Journal of the American Academy of Psychoanalysis* 13:317–328.

_____ (1986). Object constancy, object permanency, and personality disorders. In: *Self and Object Constancy: Clinical and Theoretical Perspectives,* ed. R. Lax, S. Bach, and J. A. Burland, pp. 193–207. New York: Guilford Press.

_____ (1987). A reconsideration of Fairbairn's "original object" and "original ego" in relation to borderline and other self disorders. In: *The Borderline Patient: Emerging Concepts in Diagnosis, Psychodynamics, and Treatment*, ed. J. S. Grotstein, M. F. Solomon, and J. A. Lang, vol. 1, pp. 219–231. Hillsdale, NJ: Analytic Press.

_____ (1988a). The Dipsas revisited: Comments on addiction and personality. *Journal of Substance Abuse Treatment* 5:1–7.

_____ (1988b). A review of the pathogenesis of borderline and narcissistic personality disorders. *Adolescent Psychiatry* 15:387–406.

_____ (1988c). Fairbairn's "basic endopsychic situation" considered in terms of "classical" and "deficit" metapsychological models. *Journal of the American Academy of Psychoanalysis* 16:461–477.

_____ (1989). Notes on the developmental pathogenesis of narcissistic personality disorder. *Psychiatric Clinics of North America* 12:695–708.

_____ (1990). The severely disturbed adolescent: Hospital and residential treatment. *Bulletin of the Menninger Clinic* 54.

Rinsley, D. B., and Hall, D. D. (1962). Psychiatric hospital treatment of adolescents: Parental resistances as expressed in casework metaphor. *Archives of General Psychiatry* 7:286–294.

Rinsley, D. B., and Inge, G. P. (1961). Psychiatric hospital treatment of adolescents: Verbal and nonverbal resistance to treatment. *Bulletin of the Menninger Clinic* 25:249–263.

Robins, L. N. (1966). *Deviant Children Grown Up: A Sociological and Psychiatric Study of Sociopathic Personality*. Baltimore: Williams & Wilkins.

Sarnoff, C. A. (1980). Latency-age children. In: *Emotional Disorders in Children and Adolescents: Medical and Psychological Approaches to Treatment*, ed. C. P. Sholevar, R. M. Benson, *and B. J. Blinder*, pp. 283–302. New York: SP Medical and Scientific Books.

Searles, H. F. (1967). The "dedicated physician" in psychotherapy and psychoanalysis. In: *Crosscurrents in Psychiatry and Psychoanalysis*, ed. R. W. Gibson, pp. 128–143. Philadelphia: Lippincott.

————— (1979). The patient as therapist to his analyst. In: *Countertransference and Related Subjects*, pp. 380–459. Madison, CT: International Universities Press.

Singer, E. (1971). The patient aids the analyst: Some clinical and theoretical observations. In: *In the Name of Life: Essays in Honor of Erich Fromm*, ed. B. Landis and E. S. Tauber, pp. 56–68. New York: Holt, Rinehart & Winston.

Slovenko, R. (1980). Law and psychiatry. In *Comprehensive Textbook of Psychiatry/III*, ed. H. I. Kaplan, A. F. Freedman, and B. J. Sadock, 3rd ed. vol. 3, pp. 3043–3083. Baltimore: Williams & Wilkins.

Slovenko, R., and Grossman, M. (1988). Confidentiality and testimonial privilege. In: *Psychiatry* (Looseleaf), ed. R. Michels and J. O. Cavenar, rev. ed., vol. 3, chap. 31, pp. 1–18. Philadelphia and New York: Lippincott and Basic Books.

Speers, R. W., and Morter, D. C. (1980). Overindividuation and underseparation in the pseudomature child. In: *Rapprochement: The Critical Subphase of Separation-Individuation*, ed. R. F. Lax, S. Bach, and J. A. Burland, pp. 457–477. New York: Jason Aronson.

Spitz, R. A. (1957). *No and Yes: On the Genesis of Human Communication*. New York: International Universities Press.

Stern, D. N. (1985). *The Interpersonal World of the Infant: A View From Psychoanalysis and Developmental Psychology*. New York: Basic Books.

Stone, M. H. (1980). *The Borderline Syndromes: Constitution, Personality, and Adaptation*. New York: McGraw-Hill.

Teicholz, J. G. (1978). A selective review of the psychoanalytic literature on theoretical conceptualizations of narcissism. *Journal of the American Psychoanalytic Association* 25:805–834.

Tucker, G. J., and Pincus, J. M. (1980). Child, adolescent, and adult antisocial and dyssocial behavior. In: *Comprehensive Textbook of Psychiatry/III*, ed. H. I. Kaplan, A. M. Freedman, and B. J. Sadock, 3rd ed. vol. 3, pp. 2816–2827. Baltimore: Williams & Wilkins.

Voth, H. M. (1972). Responsibility in the practice of psychoanalysis and psychotherapy. *American Journal of Psychotherapy* 26:69–83.

Whitaker, C. A., and Malone, T. P. (1953). *The Roots of Psychotherapy.* New York: Blakiston.

Winnicott, D. W. (1950–1955). Aggression in relation to emotional development. In: *Collected Papers: Through Paediatrics to Psycho-Analysis*, pp. 204–218. London: Tavistock.

———— (1951). Transitional objects and transitional phenomena. In: *Collected Papers: Through Paediatrics to Psycho-Analysis*, pp. 229–242. London: Tavistock.

———— (1960). Ego distortion in terms of true and false self. In: *The Maturational Processes and the Facilitating Environment: Studies in the Theory of Emotional Development*, pp. 140–152. New York: International Universities Press, 1965.

———— (1965). *The Maturational Processes and the Facilitating Environment: Studies in the Theory of Emotional Development.* New York: International Universities Press.

Wolberg, L. R. (1977). Supervision of the psychotherapeutic process. In: *The Technique of Psychotherapy*, 3rd ed. part (vol.) 2, pp. 936–958. New York: Grune & Stratton.

Index